T0311519

Cambridge Elements ≡

Elements in the Economics of Emerging Markets
edited by
Bruno S. Sergi
Harvard University

BRICS AND THE GLOBAL FINANCIAL ORDER

Liberalism Contested?

Johannes Petry
Goethe University Frankfurt
Andreas Nölke
Goethe University Frankfurt

CAMBRIDGE
UNIVERSITY PRESS

Shaftesbury Road, Cambridge CB2 8EA, United Kingdom

One Liberty Plaza, 20th Floor, New York, NY 10006, USA

477 Williamstown Road, Port Melbourne, VIC 3207, Australia

314–321, 3rd Floor, Plot 3, Splendor Forum, Jasola District Centre, New Delhi – 110025, India

103 Penang Road, #05–06/07, Visioncrest Commercial, Singapore 238467

Cambridge University Press is part of Cambridge University Press & Assessment, a department of the University of Cambridge.

We share the University's mission to contribute to society through the pursuit of education, learning and research at the highest international levels of excellence.

www.cambridge.org
Information on this title: www.cambridge.org/9781009498760

DOI: 10.1017/9781009498739

First published 2024

A catalogue record for this publication is available from the British Library.

ISBN 978-1-009-49876-0 Hardback
ISBN 978-1-009-49875-3 Paperback
ISSN 2631-8598 (online)
ISSN 2631-858X (print)

Cambridge University Press & Assessment has no responsibility for the persistence or accuracy of URLs for external or third-party internet websites referred to in this publication and does not guarantee that any content on such websites is, or will remain, accurate or appropriate.

BRICS and the Global Financial Order

Liberalism Contested?

Elements in the Economics of Emerging Markets

DOI: 10.1017/9781009498739
First published online: June 2024

Johannes Petry
Goethe University Frankfurt

Andreas Nölke
Goethe University Frankfurt

Author for correspondence: Johannes Petry, j.petry@soz.uni-frankfurt.de

Abstract: The global financial system is the economic bedrock of the contemporary liberal economic order. Contrary to other global-economy areas, finance is rarely analyzed in discussions on contestations of economic liberalism. However, a quite comprehensive process of external contestation of the global financial order (GFO) is underway. This contestation occurs through the rising share of emerging market economies within global finance in recent years, especially the rise of the BRICS economies. This Element investigates whether and how the BRICS contest the contemporary GFO by conducting a systematic empirical analysis across seven countries, eleven issue areas and three dimensions. This contestation occurs across issue areas but is mostly concentrated on the domestic and transnational dimension, not the international level on which much research focuses. Rather than the entire BRICS, it is especially China, Russia and India that contest liberal finance. This title is also available as Open Access on Cambridge Core.

Keywords: emerging markets, global finance, liberal international order, state capitalism, RICS, China, India, Russia, Brazil, South Africa

ISBNs: 9781009498760 (HB), 9781009498753 (PB), 9781009498739 (OC)
ISSNs: 2631-8598 (online), 2631-858X (print)

Contents

1 Introduction: The Liberal Global Financial Order and Its State-Capitalist Alternative

Since the beginning of the Ukraine war, we can observe the emergence of changing constellations within the global financial system. Western financial sanctions are targeted at Russia and (to a lesser degree) China, but there are also moves by emerging markets to evade these sanctions accompanied by more non-Western financial cooperation. From intensified economic and financial ties, gradual de-dollarization in bilateral financial activities or the potential rise of the (petro) yuan, emerging markets – especially the BRICS – are creating alternative financial spaces that provide them with a greater degree of autonomy vis-à-vis the liberal, US-dominated global financial order (GFO). Rather than tactical maneuvering, we argue that this is part of a broader and already ongoing contestation of the liberal GFO through the BRICS that has hitherto not been sufficiently analyzed in economics and political economy scholarship.[1] As we show in this Element, over time, we can observe significant and increasing divergence of national financial systems as well as contestation of the global financial institutions stemming from the BRICS and their growing importance in the global financial system.

This also has broader political implications. The global financial system is the economic bedrock of the contemporary liberal international order (LIO). Economic liberalism is a key feature of this order, next to liberal internationalism and political liberalism (Lake et al., 2021). A key turning point within economic liberalism was the shift from the postwar "embedded liberalism" (Ruggie, 1982) – for example, characterized by the Bretton Woods system – to the "neoliberal" order that has been in place since the 1980s, marked by the liberalization and internationalization of global financial activity and the subsequently increasing power of transnational financial markets (Blyth, 2012; Helleiner, 1995; Kirshner, 1999; Konings, 2016). Finance thus plays a key role within the contemporary global economy and international order.

Given its centrality for the liberal order, it is surprising that finance is hardly systematically analyzed in recent debates about its contestations (see Goddard et al., 2024; Lake et al., 2021). One of the reasons for this omission probably stems from the fact that there has been much less overt and visible contestation of the latter if compared to other elements of the economic order, at least during the last decade. Even the 2008 Global Financial Crisis (GFC) did not lead to a lasting contestation of the global order of finance; the Occupy movement died

---

[1] We define contestations as "a social practice [that] entails objection to specific issues that matter to people" (Wiener, 2014, 3); in the case of international order, these can be both discursive and behavioral practices that challenge the authority of international institutions, their intrusiveness or the liberal order as a whole (Börzel & Zürn, 2021, 288).

down quickly and postcrisis regulation did not lead to fundamental change (Helleiner, 2014; Moschella & Tsingou, 2013). Populist parties in northern economies, for instance, rather complain about the relocation of jobs in the global value chain expansion supported by trade liberalization and the ICT revolution than about the effects of financial liberalization (Broz et al., 2021; Goldstein & Gulotti, 2021; Mansfield & Rudra, 2021). Nevertheless, the relative neglect of finance in discussions about contestations of the liberal order is problematic. As we show in this Element, there is a comprehensive external contestation of the GFO underway. This contestation has to be seen against the backdrop of the rising importance and growing share of emerging market economies (EMEs) within global finance in recent years. Here, the BRICS stand out.

First, these countries belong to the largest emerging markets in the world. Between 1990 and 2020, the BRICS' contribution to global GDP grew from 7.9% to 24.7%. Measured in terms of purchasing power parity, their combined GDP even surpassed the G7 (32% vs. 30%). More importantly, they also account for an ever-greater share of global financial markets. In 2020, for instance, they accounted for 53.9% of global futures trading and 23.1% of global stock market capitalization, up from 4% and 5% respectively in 2000 (Figure 1). Analyzing their integration and the impact of their rise on the global financial system is thus an important issue.

Second, the BRICS countries are correspondingly increasingly integrated, with intra-BRICS trade surging 56% to USD 422 billion between 2017 and 2022 alone. Importantly, this non-Western alliance is bound to become even

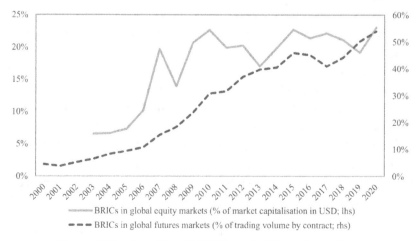

Figure 1 The rise of the BRICS in global financial markets.
Source: *WFE, FIA; author's calculation (data for China includes Hong Kong).*

more important economically through its planned inclusion of some of the world's largest oil producers in 2024. Although China has by far the largest economic and political weight in the BRICS grouping, a *collective* contestation by the BRICS group definitely has more weight as it has the potential for creating alternative multilateral institutions (Roberts et al., 2018). This relates not only to the number of countries and their combined share of the global economy but also to their internal heterogeneity in terms of political systems (democracies and autocracies), as well as to the latent geopolitical conflicts between some of their members (e.g. China and India).

Third, as we demonstrate in this Element, the core of the BRICS challenge is not only on the level of international institutions but primarily the successful establishment of alternative financial systems on the national level and their transnational expansion. A GFO does not only consist of global institutions but also pertains to how financial systems are organized on the national level. Moreover, we always need to study the transnational relations between national units. Contestation can take place on only one, two or all three of these levels. Therefore, our focus on the BRICS grouping is only partially due to their establishment of international institutions, but we primarily focus on the BRICS' domestic financial systems and their transnational expansion.

Fourth, although the BRICS have not yet become a cohesive economic actor, they nonetheless serve as an important rallying point for large EMEs. This does not necessarily mean that the BRICS member states act in a concerted effort. However, especially with respect to economic topics, they are still the only major symbolic alternative to Western-led clubs such as the G7 or OECD, and their role in contesting the liberal order has repeatedly been invoked (Ban & Blyth, 2013; Chin, 2014; Liu & Papa, 2022). As a *Bloomberg* report (Hancock & Cohen, 2023) put it, "the BRICS group of emerging market nations ... has gone from a slogan dreamed up at an investment bank two decades ago to a real-world club that controls a multilateral lender" that is "promoting a move toward a more 'multipolar' world and away from the post-Cold War dominance of the US." Finance has thereby been a central issue area. In fact, the first joint statement from the inaugural 2009 BRICs Summit in Yekaterinburg – often seen as the group's "founding document" (Stuenkel, 2020, 188) – explicitly focuses on reforming the GFO after the GFC provided the impulse for the group's initial formation and continued integration.

Finally, the BRICS are increasingly gaining momentum as a political entity. With Saudi Arabia, Egypt, the United Arab Emirates (UAE), Iran and Ethiopia, five new members have been admitted to this non-Western club on January 1, 2024. This BRICS+ group now accounts for 29% of global GDP, 46% of the global population, 25% of global exports and 43% of global oil production

(Lu, 2023). Especially with respect to the importance of oil trading for the global dominance of the USD, the BRICS expansion also has important potential implications for the global financial system (see Section 5). With more and more countries expressing their interest in joining the group, exploring the BRICS' impact on global finance is an important research area.

Importantly, in terms of their economic systems, there are important commonalities between BRICS member states (Nölke et al., 2020). The state has a much larger role in steering economic activity, which is often discussed under the term state capitalism in the comparative capitalism literature (Alami & Dixon, 2020; Kurlantzick, 2016; Musacchio & Lazzarini, 2013; Naughton & Tsai, 2015; Nölke et al., 2020). While these economies broadly follow capitalist principles, their differing institutional setup facilitates different socioeconomic outcomes than more liberal forms of capitalism (Feldmann, 2019; Hall and Soskice, 2001; Jackson and Deeg, 2008). This applies especially to their financial systems as one crucial institutional sphere within their national economies (Allen and Gale, 2000; Petry et al., 2023).[2] An important question is therefore whether to adapt to the liberal, US-dominated GFO or whether can they potentially contest the contemporary order. In this Element, we demonstrate that this development is not only an issue of divergent domestic economic systems but also of transnational expansion and of contesting the international institutions that underpin the liberal GFO.

While there is an extensive literature on this topic, we argue that existing research on the contestation of the liberal GFO is limited in three ways: A large portion of existing literature focuses (1) only on China, (2) on very specific aspects of this contestation and/or (3) only on the level of international organizations. China is most often analyzed as a contestant of the liberal economic order (de Graaff et al., 2020; Hameiri & Jones, 2018; Weiss & Wallace, 2021). With respect to finance, prominent topics are thereby the evolution of China's role in development finance (Bräutigam, 2011; Chin & Gallagher, 2019), the establishment of new China-led multilateral development banks such as the AIIB (Cammack, 2018; Wang, 2019; Yu, 2017), RMB internationalization (Cohen, 2012, 2019; Helleiner & Kirschner, 2014; McNally & Gruin, 2017; Subacchi, 2018) or the internationalization of Chinese finance and capital (Kaplan, 2021; ten Brink, 2015; Petry, 2023; Zhu, 2018).

Other research has focused on other BRICS countries – researching, for instance, cross-border finance in South Africa and Brazil (Alami, 2020), capital controls in Brazil, India and China (Abdelal, 2007; Dierckx, 2013) or

---

[2] To be sure, this juxtaposition only serves to identify differences between financial systems, not about alternatives to capitalism or economic growth or the globalization of finance more broadly.

Russia's financial opening (Logvinenko, 2021) – while others have analyzed the BRICS group as a whole (e.g. Batista, 2022; Gallagher, 2015; Roberts et al., 2018). However, often these empirical analyses only focus on specific areas such as credit rating agencies (Helleiner & Wang, 2018), capital mobility (Gallagher, 2015), capital markets (Petry et al., 2023), development finance (Ban & Blyth, 2013) or currencies (Liu & Papa, 2022); they focus on the creation of new international financial institutions (IFIs) such as the BRICS New Development Bank (NewDB; Chin, 2014; Griffith-Jones, 2014; Hooijmaaijers, 2021; Wang, 2019) and Contingent Reserve Arrangement (CRA; Bond, 2016; Ocampo, 2017) and/or on the BRICS' influence on existing IFIs (Batista, 2022; Grabel, 2017). Importantly, a majority of this research focuses on the level of international institutions, regimes and organization and neglects other potential channels of contestation (also Huotari & Hanemann, 2014).

What is missing is a *systematic* analysis of the BRICS' contestation of the GFO. Often, existing studies make broad generalizations about implications for the GFO in general, based on the study of very specific issues, while others only provide insights on individual aspects. This entails the danger of overplaying the degree of contestation, if research is focused on prominent cases of contestation (as, e.g. in development financing) and thereby ignores cases of non-contestation. At the same time, there is also the risk of underestimating contestation if studies extrapolate from one case where contestation failed (as, e.g. in credit rating). Even more problematical, existing literature is quite vague when defining the GFO, its liberal elements and non-liberal alternatives. Usually, the focus is simply on the policy initiatives of specific countries (mostly China) in selected issue areas, without considerations of the broader implications for the GFO. In addition, existing research tends to focus on the level of international organizations, neglecting domestic and transnational mechanisms of GFO contestation (see Section 1.1). The overarching objective of this Element is therefore to assess whether, how and why the BRICS contest the liberal GFO in a more systematic way.

In order to demonstrate the increasing degree of external contestation of the liberal GFO, our Element pursues a systematic approach, both conceptually and empirically (with a focus on the latter). Conceptually, the Element answers the following questions:

- What is the GFO and how can it be contested?
- Which issue areas belong to the GFO?
- What is liberal about the contemporary GFO?
- What is the alternative to the liberal GFO?

Empirically, this Element analyzes the varieties of contestation of the liberal GFO:

- Where is the liberal GFO contested (in which issue areas and about which principles)?
- Who contests the liberal GFO (which states)?
- Through which mechanisms is the liberal GFO contested (via domestic alternatives, transnational spread of alternatives or alternative international institutions)?

Overall, our empirical analysis demonstrates a surprisingly clear ordering, with China, India and Russia at the state-capitalist pole, the US and the UK at the liberal pole, and Brazil and South Africa as mixed cases in between. Further, the GFO is contested across issue areas albeit to varying degrees and most contestation occurs at the domestic and transnational levels, not so much at the international level – on which most existing literature has focused. While the BRICS might find it challenging to jointly organize alternative multilateral institutions, we can definitely observe an increasing transnational spread of their state-capitalist financial practices. Our study thereby provides a comprehensive assessment of the external contestation of the liberal GFO.

1.1 Conceptual Framework

In order to study the contestation of the liberal GFO systematically, we answer four conceptual questions. First, we clarify what the GFO is, and how it could be contested. Second, we establish which issue areas are parts of the GFO. Third, we highlight what is liberal about the contemporary GFO. Fourth, we detail what the potential EME alternative to a GFO is, in particular with regard to its non-liberal, state-capitalist features. Existing literature does not address these questions comprehensively. Correspondingly, some of our clarifications should also be relevant for studying the economic implications of the rise of EMEs outside of finance.

First, what is a global (financial) order? Existing literature gives rather vague answers to this question (Adler-Nissen & Zarakol, 2021; Börzel & Zürn, 2021; Farrell & Newman, 2021; Flaherty & Rogowski, 2021; Lake et al., 2021; Simmons & Goemans, 2021). However, a basic common understanding of many studies is that an international order implicitly consists of three elements: international institutions, domestic features and the stream of interactions across borders (e.g. Adler-Nissen & Zarakol, 2021, 612–613; Farrell & Newman, 2021, 33; Paul, 2021, 1605; Weiss & Wallace, 2021, 636–637).

A global economic order does therefore not only consist of the global institutions that usually are studied by international political economy (IPE) but also pertains to how the economy is organized on the national level, the focus of studies in comparative political economy (CPE). Moreover, we always need to study the interdependence between national units as well, a crucial aspect that tends to be forgotten in the often too strict sharing of tasks between the two disciplines that focus either on the international level or on the comparison of national economies (Farrell & Newman, 2014).[3] Consequently, this means that any systematic study of the financial aspects of global order requires a combination of IPE and CPE to study its constitutive aspects: (1) the types of capitalism on the national level; (2) the transnational interdependencies between these different capitalisms; (3) international institutions and conflicts about regulation on the global level.

We define contestation as "both discursive and behavioral practices that challenge the authority of international institutions, their intrusiveness, or the [liberal order] as a whole" (Börzel & Zürn, 2021, 288). Contestation can thereby take place on only one, two or all three levels of the contemporary GFO. While contestation on the domestic level is about creating alternative/autonomous spaces, the transnational level examines the expansion of these practices abroad, while the international level is the strongest form of contestation as this is where the rules and regulations for the global financial system are set. Importantly, the degree of contestation increases from the national via the transnational to the international level. The existence of, for instance, state ownership or capital controls in emerging economies is already a form of contestation, given that it contests liberal ideas of free capital flows and constricts the power of US investors that underpin the liberal economic order. However, this resistance to conform with the GFO is a less aggressive form of contestation, if compared with transnational flows, for example, via the acquisition of companies in liberal economies by state-owned companies ("transnational state capitalism," Liu and Lim 2023). The potentially most wide-ranging form of contestation then is the replacement or substantial modification of the stabilizing institutions of incumbent GFO at the international level. Existing research on contestations of the liberal GFO misses important cases of contestation because it mostly focuses on the international level. However, contestation on the second and/or the third level usually predisposes contestation on the first level: Why should you try to spread state-capitalist practices transnationally or even globally, if you do not have state capitalism at home? Thus focusing on all three levels of analysis matters. As second-image IPE has highlighted, it is crucial to analyze this interplay of national, transnational and international levels of analysis for understanding

---

[3] While there is an increasing reciprocal acknowledgment of these two literatures, they are very seldomly integrated into a coherent analytical framework (Nölke, 2011).

global political-economic phenomena (Kalinowski, 2013; Nölke, 2023; Pape & Petry, 2024). This Element therefore explores all three levels of contestation when analyzing the BRICS and their relationship toward the contemporary GFO.

Second, what are the issue areas of a GFO? Again, the absence of a clear definition seems to be a problem. Comprehensive treatments of global finance (Baker et al., 2005; Germain, 2010; Gourinchas et al. 2019; Helleiner et al., 2010; Porter, 2005) do not systematically address this question. The same applies to the more specific literature that refers to one or several GFOs (Drezner & McNamara, 2013; Germain, 2009; Huotari & Hanemann, 2014; Langley, 2003; Petry, 2021b). These literatures intuitively select central issue areas of GFO for discussion, without accounting for the composition of the overall order.[4] Given this vagueness, our subsequent elaboration should also be relevant to scholars of finance in general, irrespective of the specific question of GFO contestation.

Our identification of issue areas of the GFO is based on the following consideration: Since finance is closely intertwined with many other economic issues, GFO needs to be broadly defined. It cannot only be studied with a narrow focus on capital markets, but it must also take into account areas such as monetary relations, investment flows or development finance. Taking this as our point of departure, we derive eleven issue areas of the GFO (Table 1), roughly grouped according to macroeconomic (monetary) and microeconomic (company finance) aspects, with some specific issues for poorer countries (development finance).[5]

On the macroeconomic side, three issue areas constitute the monetary sub-order. The first refers to exchange rate regimes (fixed or floating), including their management on the international level, for example, via the Bretton Woods System (1). A related issue is the management of the balance of payments, with the issue of reserve currencies (one or several) at its center (2). Finally, central banks and their monetary policies are also part of the monetary sub-order (3). On the microeconomic side, six issue areas constitute the (company) finance sub-order. The first two of these link the financing of companies predominantly to the international level, with different time horizons. As previously mentioned, international capital mobility – in particular the absence of national capital controls – is a core pillar of the liberal GFO (4). Whereas capital controls

---

[4] Only within the more specific literature on the global monetary sub-order we find a slightly more systematic reflection on its composition, i.e. "reserve currencies, international financial institutions, and central banks" (Norrlof et al., 2020, 109).

[5] While we analyze offshore finance in various sections (exchange rate regimes and capital mobility), we do not focus on offshore tax havens since this is largely an issue of fiscal policy. Similarly, we do not focus on illicit financial flows as we are concerned with institutionalised and regulated aspects of global finance.

Table 1 Issue areas of the global financial order.

Global financial order	
Monetary sub-order	Exchange rate regimes
	Balance of payments
	Monetary policy
Financial sub-order	International capital mobility
	Foreign direct investment
	Corporate ownership and governance
	Banks and banking regulations
	Financial markets
	Accounting standards
Development sub-order	International debt management
	Development finance

Source: *Authors' table.*

are particularly important for short-term portfolio investments, they also matter for more long-term foreign direct investment (FDI), their management via bilateral investment treaties (BITs) as well as investor-state arbitration panels (5). Another important dimension is the issue of corporate ownership and governance, including the rise of institutional investors such as pension funds, hedge funds, private equity and also state ownership or sovereign wealth funds (SWFs) (6). Companies mobilize new funding either via banks or via financial markets – two important aspects of GFOs. Correspondingly, we need to study banks and banking regulations (7) as well as several aspects of the financial markets (for assets such as stocks, bonds and derivatives) and their regulation (8). Finally, company finance also requires accounting standards, which enable the valuation of companies and their assets (9). Finally, low-income economies face specific challenges that also have to be reflected in any GFO. On the short-term macroeconomic level, continuing balance-of-payment problems lead to international indebtedness, which is managed by a set of debtor institutions (Paris Club, London Club) including the International Monetary Fund (IMF) and its adjustment programs (10). Next to the issue of short-term balance-of-payment problems and mid-term government indebtedness, developing countries also require more long-term project financing, which can come from very different sources and may be provided under quite different conditions (11).

Third, having established which areas constitute a GFO, we need to establish what is liberal about the contemporary GFO. The frequent complaint about the "vagueness" of discussions about the contestation of the liberal order is not only related to the problem of how to define a global order but also to how we define "liberal." Still, there is a somewhat higher degree of convergence on its definition if compared with the conceptualization of global orders. Very broadly, the liberal order consists of economic liberalism, political liberalism and liberal internationalism (Lake et al., 2021), as a "rules-based order that privileges democracy, free enterprise, and individual political freedoms" (Weiss & Wallace, 2021, 639). However, these are not yet operational concepts, and we need to operationalize "liberal" for specific global sub-orders. Here we can draw on existing research. Drezner and McNamara (2013), for instance, highlight that GFOs can be characterized by studying the underlying ideas and power structures (Barma & Weber, 2007, 25). However, we need to add a third element, institutions, as every economy consists of a set of institutions that create distinct patterns of constraints and incentives that shape and channel actors' behaviors (Zysman, 1994, 245–246). Institutions reflect and stabilize ideas and power structures in the longer term.

What now are the specific ideas, power structures and institutions that characterize the liberal GFO – or more specifically its neoliberal form that has been established since the 1980s? Liberal ideas on the macro level focus on free cross-border capital flows. On the micro level, the central idea of a liberal GFO is to allow the private owners of companies to pursue their profit motive without public restrictions, which under conditions of financialization means allowing for the maximization of shareholder value. In terms of microlevel institutions, liberalism entails a preference for light public regulation by the state or private self-regulation by financial market actors. On the macro-institutional level, in contrast, there is a preference for powerful international institutions that facilitate high cross-border integration and liquidity. Correspondingly, there is a clear contrast between the need for centralized financial institutions globally and rather hands-off institutions domestically.

Next to ideas and institutions, power structures are the third important element for the identification of a global order. Without any doubt, the US played a crucial role in the establishment of the current liberal economic order (Helleiner, 1996; McDowell, 2016),[6] although the current GFO is jointly led with the UK (often termed Anglo-America) – and includes a prominent role for the Wall Street and the City of London, the US dollar, global (mostly Anglo-American) investors, and a set of global financial infrastructures controlled by private and public Anglo-American actors (Gabor, 2021; Green, 2020; Pape, 2022). Arguably, highly integrated and liquid financial structures – optimal for free markets and capital flows – are best organized around a powerful core. Domestically, in contrast, the preference is for (very) limited power of states

---

[6] But see Abdelal (2007) for a complementary perspective.

over finance, in order not to get into the way of financial activities. Both features – global centralization and light state control on the national level – are two sides of the same coin. Importantly, the liberal global financial system has worked very much in favor of its protagonists; as Konings (2007, 49–50) noted, "the creation of a highly integrated and liquid financial structure [has] enhanced America's structural power in international finance." US financial hegemony and liberal financial norms are very much entangled, as the global diffusion of (neo)liberal finance very much reproduces and reinforces US power.

Fourth, now that we have established what constitutes the "liberal" GFO, what is its theoretical alternative? While this is a difficult definitory task, arguably most observations of contestation agree on the idea of a high degree of state protection and sovereignty as an alternative to economic liberalism where the latter is often circumscribed. Contestations of economic liberalism by powers such as China and Russia focus on state sovereignty (Börzel & Zürn, 2021; Farrell & Newman, 2021; Roberts et al., 2019). This focus on state sovereignty does not mean an absence of international cooperation; it rather means to "manage international politics through a neo-Westphalian synthesis comprised of hard-shell states that bargain with each other about the terms of their external relationships, but staunchly respect the rights of each other to order its own society, politics and culture without external interference" (Barma et al., 2007, 25).

Based on these general considerations, we can derive some more specific considerations on the ideas and institutions supporting a statist GFO, as an alternative to the liberal one. The core idea on the macro level is the protection of national sovereignty, especially against cross-border financial flows as a particularly aggressive form of liberal intrusiveness, which is institutionally supported by creating alternative international organizations or by weakening the intrusive character of existing ones. Especially in a context of US financial hegemony that is further bolstered through liberal finance, protecting national sovereignty becomes an evermore urgent task. In case of the "liberal" GFO, we hence argue that its theoretical alternative would constitute a "state-capitalist" one. Here we can draw on a recent literature that has studied the financial systems of especially non-Western economies under this heading (Alami & Dixon, 2020; Musacchio & Lazzarini, 2013; Naughton & Tsai, 2015; Nölke et al., 2020; Petry et al., 2021b). Which ideas, power structures and institutions characterize contemporary state capitalism – and by implications a state-capitalist GFO – in an ideal typical way? In contrast to popular perceptions, contemporary state capitalism is not primarily about direct state ownership of individual companies but about state control over the economy.

On the micro level, the core principle is the protection of national policy space, institutionally supported by a maximization of state capacity. This means having a financial system whose institutions support processes of catch-up industrialization and implement limits on the ability of private profit maximization (if this stands in conflict national development objectives), often involving restrictions that impede the maximization of shareholder value and instead facilitate the accomplishment of state objectives. All of this takes place under conditions of globally liberalized financial markets. With respect to power structures, the state is the most powerful entity on the national level, while internationally we expect a preference for nonintrusive multilateral institutions that do not impede national sovereignty.[7]

Interestingly, there are some common points of the state-capitalist challenge to economic liberalism with the predecessor of the contemporary liberal financial order, that is, the post–World War II compromise of embedded liberalism (Ruggie, 1982). Under embedded liberalism, powerful national governments closely circumscribed both the freedom of finance on the domestic level and cross-border financial flows. A state-capitalist financial order would arguably allow for a return toward a higher degree of embeddedness. However, both the liberal GFO and its state-capitalist challenger take place under conditions of financialization.[8] The current alternative to liberal financialization is not de-financialization (a complete return to embedded liberalism) but state-capitalist financialization (Petry et al., 2021b).

Overall, the conceptual apparatus based on these elements allows for a systematic study of the increasing external contestation of the contemporary GFO. For each issue area of the latter, we can derive the liberal incumbent as well as the state-capitalist alternative, assisted by the three levels of potential contestation.

1.2 Empirical Approach

After developing the conceptual apparatus for studying contestation of the GFO, empirically the question then is (1) whether contestation takes place, in which issue areas and by which countries; (2) whether it is limited to the domestic level or spreads to the more aggressive forms of contestation on the transnational or international level and (3) whether it increases over time.

---

[7] While we are aware of the abstraction and simplification that our heuristic dichotomy implies, we consider it important for analytical parsimony; these ideal types are used as a guiding heuristic for the nuanced systematic empirical analysis of this Element.

[8] " ... financialization means the increasing role of financial motives, financial markets, financial actors and financial institutions in the operation of the domestic and international economies" (Epstein, 2005, 3).

In the following sections, we systematically analyze the BRICS across the eleven identified issue areas of the GFO and whether they follow liberal or state-capitalist logic across domestic, transnational and international dimensions and are thus contesting the liberal GFO (or not). We contrast the data on the BRICS with the US and UK, as the core of the incumbent liberal order. Given the Anglo-American dominance within the contemporary GFO, it is far more instructive to compare the BRICS as potential contestants with these two core countries than with other major economies like Germany and Japan, which arguably play a less important role within global finance (Fichtner, 2017; Oatley et al., 2013).[9] Empirically, our study thus examines the contestation of the liberal GFO by state capitalism through a comparative analysis of these seven countries across eleven issue areas and three levels of potential contestation – the domestic, transnational and international levels. We thereby focus on the period from 2000 to 2023[10] in which we can observe the rise of the BRICS and their potential contestation of the liberal GFO following the AFC.

To comprehensively analyze these 231 datapoints, our analysis combines insights from secondary literature, policy documents and financial data.[11] First, we review the secondary literature on different aspects of GFO contestation. Second, we analyze policy documents, regulatory frameworks and research reports on individual countries and issue areas. Third, we compile an extensive dataset with both qualitative and quantitative financial data drawing on Bloomberg Terminal data, various financial industries associations and standard setting bodies, international organizations as well as national central banks, statistic bureaus and regulators.[12]

In our conclusion, we then use heat maps to summarize and visualize the complex results of our empirical analysis. As Wilke (2019) noted, heat maps do "an excellent job of highlighting broader trends," especially for larger, more

---

[9] While the financial systems of countries like France or Japan are less liberal than those of the US or UK, which would add more nuance to our analysis (Hall and Soskice, 2001; Karwowski et al., 2020), given the centrality of Anglo-America for the contemporary GFO, we only focus on these liberal benchmarks against which to assess the rise of the BRICS; see also Section 5.

[10] However, some data is only available until 2021 or 2022.

[11] There is of course a tradeoff as we cannot conduct an in-depth/nuanced analysis when aiming to provide a systematic overview across these different issue areas.

[12] Some of this analysis is based on primary data like analyzing ownership patterns by investor types (Section 3.3) or the accumulation of FX reserves (Section 2.2), while other parts of the analysis rely on indices like the Chinn–Ito Financial Openness Index (Section 3.1) or OECD FDI Regulatory Restrictiveness Index (Section 3.2). On the one hand, these indices provide a good overview of individual issue areas, which is helpful given the variety of issue areas that this Element addresses. On the other hand, the condensation of complex topics like restrictions on FDI flows into simple numerical tools of course neglect nuances within individual country regimes. However, given the breadth of the issue areas covered in this Element, in-depth analyses of individual issue areas were not possible. Our approach was thus to use primary data where possible and only revert to well-established indices like the aforementioned.

complex datasets. In our case, heat maps allow us to illustrate (1) whether and to what extent countries engage in contestation, (2) in which issue areas this contestation is most pronounced and (3) on which level the contestation of the GFO is strongest.

Based on our analysis of individual issue areas, we create individual heat maps for the domestic, transnational and international levels of contestation; each heat map consisting of seven columns (one for each country case) and at least eleven rows (at least one row for each issue area). Drawing on our previous analysis, each cell then contains empirical findings in the form of a numerical or ordinal value with the specific countries' characteristics for the respective issue area.[13] Each row is then color-coded depending on whether these values align more closely with liberal or state-capitalist ideal types. Since we are looking at the continuum between two conceptual ideal types, we use a bivariate color scheme. The more state-capitalist a country is, the darker its coloring. For corporate ownership, for instance, we posit that 0% state ownership of listed companies corresponds with the liberal ideal type, while 100% corresponds with the state-capitalist ideal type. Importantly, heat maps "rely fundamentally on . . . meaningful reordering of the rows and columns" (Gehlenborg & Wong, 2012), which is why we then hierarchically cluster rows and columns according to similarity (i.e. where countries stand on the liberal/state-capitalist continuum as well as the overall degree of contestedness of individual issue areas).

Overall, these heat maps demonstrate a surprisingly clear ordering, with China, India and Russia at the state-capitalist pole, the US and the UK at the liberal pole, and Brazil and South Africa as mixed cases in between. Thereby, our study provides a comprehensive assessment of the external contestation of economic liberalism through EMEs – especially China, Russia and India – with respect to finance.

2 Contestation of the Monetary Sub-order

In the following empirical analysis, we systematically investigate whether the BRICS follow liberal or state-capitalist principles across the eleven identified GFO issue areas and across domestic, transnational and international levels of contestation. This first section focuses on macroeconomic issues that constitute the GFO's monetary sub-order, analyzing (1) exchange rate regimes and their international management, (2) the balance of payments, which is largely focused on the question of reserve currencies as well as (3) the role of central banks and their monetary policies within the GFO.

---

[13] If data in the detailed empirical analyses are not immediately observable as numerical values, they will be transformed using a coding scheme (as outlined in the discussion of each heat map).

2.1 Exchange Rate Regimes

The system between foreign exchange (FX) rates is a fundamental building block of GFOs. In the contemporary liberal GFO, exchange rates are supposed to be solely determined by market prices ("free-float"). In contrast, a state-capitalist logic prescribes managing exchange rates ("managed"), with state interventions into an otherwise market-based exchange rate representing an interim category ("float").

As an analysis of the IMF's *Annual Report on Exchange Arrangements and Exchange Restrictions* (IMF, 2021) highlights, we can thereby observe significant variation when it comes to *domestic* FX regimes. Corresponding with the liberal ideal type, the US and UK have had freely floating exchange rates since the collapse of Bretton Woods. In contrast, from the perspective of a state-capitalist ideal type, we would expect the FX regime to be managed to preserve the policy autonomy of state authorities. Brazil and South Africa are categorized as floating regimes with some rather infrequent exchange rate interventions. Interestingly, both countries switched from a managed to a floating regime in 1999 and 1998, respectively, as a response to the 1997–1998 financial crises (Mminele, 2013, 319; Ayres et al., 2019, 21). India also has a floating regime but with much more frequent exchange rate interventions where "episodes of volatility were effectively managed through timely monetary and administrative measures" (Dua & Ranjan, 2012) and has often been described as a managed floating regime. Since 2013, Russia had ceased any currency manipulation, submitting to a free-float regime, before reimposing currency controls after the Ukraine invasion in 2022, and we have since seen a reversal toward a managed FX regime (Davis et al., 2022). China, finally, has a managed exchange rate whose price may fluctuate within a ±2% band against a basket of major currencies, necessitating very frequent market interventions (Das, 2019). While this constitutes a move away from a previously fixed exchange rate system that was in place until 2005, this is a reflection of China having to operate under the conditions of financialization rather than a retreat of state-capitalist principles as "distinct measures of state control over the exchange rate ... are retained" (McNally & Gruin, 2017, 607). While Brazil, like many other countries, had also been accused of currency manipulation by president Trump, India and China are actually included in the US Treasury currency manipulator watch list due to their frequent FX interventions.[14] Overall, when it comes to domestic exchange rate systems, we can see contestation of liberal

---

[14] See https://home.treasury.gov/policy-issues/international/macroeconomic-and-foreign-exchange-policies-of-major-trading-partners-of-the-united-states.

principles from India, China and more recently Russia, while Brazil and South Africa have early on adopted liberal principles.

This is not only restricted to the domestic context but also has a transnational dimension. Liberal logic promoted large and liquid offshore currency markets that further facilitate market-based FX rate systems. However, from a state-capitalist perspective, offshore currency markets should be restricted since they reduce the state's capacity for exchange rate intervention. As a private authority that defines global criteria for market accessibility based on a liberal playbook (Petry et al., 2021a), index provider MSCI assesses the extent of such restrictions in its *Global Market Accessibility Reviews* (MSCI, 2010, 2020, 2023).

In these reviews, MSCI reports "no issues" (++), "no major issues, improvements possible" (+) or that "improvements are needed" (–/?) for individual countries. Since MSCI started its reporting in 2010, the US, UK and South Africa thereby follow liberal principles by enabling and facilitating liquid and efficient offshore market (++). While Russia had moved closer to liberal principles after 2010, reporting no major issues (+) besides an undeveloped offshore currency market and consequently most FX transactions being settled onshore, this radically changed in 2022. After an upgrade (+ to ++) in 2021, Russia was downgraded to the lowest category following Western financial sanctions and countermoves by the government to tighten control over the financial system in 2022. For Brazil and India, MSCI notes that current conditions do not satisfy liberal criteria (–/?) since there are no offshore currency markets for their currencies and that there are significant constraints on onshore currency markets (e.g. that FX transactions must be linked to security transactions). Importantly, this has not changed over time as governments hold on to the capacity to manage their currencies. In contrast, China is rated as increasingly facilitating offshore currency markets in recent years (+). Importantly, however, China is thereby not converging with liberal norms but rather engages in a controlled financial opening to promote the internationalization of the RMB as a global currency. While departing from the state-capitalist ideal type, the mechanisms of China's global integration continue to follow a state-capitalist logic (McNally & Gruin, 2017; Petry, 2021b).[15] Overall, we can see pressures to resist the liberal principle of establishing offshore currency markets in India and Brazil, China establishing them in a controlled way, Russia as a more volatile case and South Africa remaining staunchly in the liberal camp.

---

[15] Hong Kong accounts for 75% of all offshore RMB trading and 89% of RMB cross-border settlement (FSDC, 2019), an arrangement that is purposefully facilitated by Chinese authorities as it allows internationalization via Chinese-controlled Hong Kong while maintaining control over offshore currency markets.

This issue leads us to the level of international institutions and policy coordination, where the core issue of contention is dollar hegemony. The question thereby is whether to leave the issue of lead currencies to market forces (and existing power structures) as in the liberal GFO, which facilitate the dominance of one key currency that enables efficient financial transactions, or whether to reduce USD-dependence through conscious steps toward a more multipolar currency system (state-capitalist GFO).

China is thereby the most important BRICS contestant of the international institutions that underpin the FX rate system in the GFO – namely the post-Bretton Woods system of floating exchange rates that is anchored around the USD as the global reserve currency. Especially since the GFC, China has been very active in calling for a more multipolar currency system and has started facilitating the internationalization of the renminbi. While other BRICS countries do not follow the same ambitious approach of domestic currency internationalization (also because of their smaller economic size), we can observe conscious efforts to reduce dependency on the US dollar by several BRICS countries (Liu & Papa, 2022), especially as the US has been increasingly weaponizing USD hegemony (McDowell, 2023).

While originally embedded into the USD system, since 2013, Russia has also been at the forefront of de-dollarization (McDowell, 2023) with the dollar's share in Russia's trade and financial flows dropping by 15–20% (ING, 2020). In efforts to reduce its exposure to USD markets, it, for instance, facilitated the use of domestic currencies in bilateral trading with other countries. The dollar's share in Sino-Russian trade settlement, for instance, dropped from 90% in 2015 to only 20% in 2023 (Global Times, 2023; Simes, 2020), while the dollar now only accounted for less than 50% of Russian exports to India, down from 95% in 2013 (ING, 2020). In 2021, Russia and India then announced to completely phase out the dollar in their bilateral settlements, while India itself also announced to promote its domestic currencies' use in trade settlement to reduce dollar dependency (Jiamei, 2022). China also radically increased the use of RMB. In the second quarter of 2023, the RMB accounted for 49% of China's bilateral trade, topping the dollar for the first time. In the aftermath of US sanctions following the invasion of Ukraine, China, India and Russia then agreed to take further steps toward increasing share of national currencies between members of the Shanghai Cooperation Organization (Reuters, 2022). While traditionally more in the liberal camp, with the election of the Lula government, de-dollarization efforts have also increased in Brazil. At the Paris Climate Finance in 2023, Lula for instance posed the question "why can't we trade in our own currencies?" reiterating his concerns about the negative impact of

USD dominance on developing countries.[16] In contrast, de-dollarization efforts in South Africa are rather small – it is especially the Asian BRICS members that have increasingly pushed for an alternative, multipolar currency system.

2.2 Balance of Payments

Linked to the exchange rate system is how the balance of payments between countries is managed within the global economy. Liberal logic advocates only one reserve currency (USD) based around a highly integrated and liquid market structure, secured by swap lines centered around. This setup is enforced through one central international institution (IMF) that enforces liberalization in case of crisis (structural adjustment programs; SAPs) and only issues limited special drawing rights (SDRs) in order to force countries to accept adjustment programs. In contrast, state-capitalist logic that emphasizes state capacity and intervention advocates for high reserve accumulation on the national level, a diversification of reserve currencies and an extension of swap lines/(re)financing mechanisms beyond US-centered institutions such as the Fed and IMF.

On the domestic level, this translates into two different coping mechanisms. Since it contradicts efficiency, reserve accumulation is not encouraged from a liberal perspective. From a state-capitalist perspective, reserve accumulation is instead encouraged since it enables the state to utilize these assets for various political purposes. Between 2000 and 2022, the US, UK and Europe, for instance, significantly reduced their FX reserves, from accounting for 2.1%, 2.3% and 14.7% of global reserves to 0.14%, 3.58% and 2.22%, respectively. Meanwhile, the BRICS increased their share from 2.87% in 2000 to 38.23% in 2022. While China accounts for most of these reserves in absolute terms (26.14%), Russia and India are still well above the West, with Brazil on the same level as Europe and South Africa similar to Anglo-America.

However, it is important to consider these figures on a relative basis. After all, the US economy is much larger than South Africa and maintaining the same absolute level of reserves is more costly for smaller economies. The relevance of reserve accumulation therefore becomes even more apparent when analyzing them as a share of the countries' national GDP. Here, the BRICS range between 13.2% and 29.96%. Importantly, in relative terms, reserve accumulation is more important for Russia (22.19%), with the other BRICS ranging between 16.91% and 17.70%. This is significantly larger than the US (0.14%), UK (3.58%) and Euro zone (2.22%). Further, we can also observe how reserve accumulation has dropped over time in Western countries both in terms of overall share as well as

---

[16] www.ft.com/content/669260a5-82a5-4e7a-9bbf-4f41c54a6143.

relative to GDP, while it massively expanded across the BRICS from accounting for 2.87% of global FX reserves and 7.95% of BRICS' GDP in 2000 to 38.23% and 17.7% in 2022, respectively. Across the BRICS, reserve accumulation has emerged as a crucial tool for managing their balance of payment, signifying a stark contestation of liberal norms (Table 2).

Since the GFC, countries have increasingly created transnational networks of swap lines between national central banks in order to counteract their balance-of-payment problems. While in 2005 only three bilateral swap lines for a total of USD6 billion existed, by 2020 that number increased to ninety-one swap lines over USD1,885 billion (Perks et al., 2021). In the liberal GFO Fed-centered swap lines have served as a powerful tool of US monetary policy, cementing the USD's role as the global reserve currency and existing power constellations (Pape, 2022). Only Brazil is part of the Fed's network and access is capped at USD60 billion, while all other BRICS economies are cut out from this network.[17]

However, in recent years, we can observe how the BRICS have increasingly created their own network of swap lines. Starting in 2009, China has created a network of thirty-one bilateral swap lines that enable countries to borrow RMB (worth RMB3,707 billion; USD567 billion), including Russia (RMB150 billion), South Africa (RMB30 billion) and Brazil (RMB30 billion). Importantly, a range of countries have been using China's swap lines to counter their balance-of-payment problems – notably Pakistan, Mongolia, Argentina, Ukraine and Turkey (Perks et al., 2021, 14). Similarly, India has established swap lines with Japan, Sri Lanka, the Maldives and the UAE and is openly discussing a bilateral swap line with Russia to circumvent Western sanctions after Russia's invasion of Ukraine (Goldman, 2022). China's existing swap line with Russia is similarly discussed as a potential avenue to circumvent sanctions (Bloomberg News, 2022a). Importantly, we can thereby also observe how the BRICS are reducing the role of the USD as a global reserve currency. On the one hand, IMF COFER data shows a decline of the US dollar as reserve currency, coinciding with the emergence of nontraditional reserve currencies (Figure 2). On the other hand, a recent IMF working paper demonstrates that we can observe the global emergence of an RMB-focused currency bloc that is centered around the BRICS economies (IMF, 2018). Between the first quarters of 2019 and 2023, for instance, central banks tripled their use of Chinese swap lines to RMB109 billion (USD

---

[17] Although they can access the Fed's FIMA repo facility, which according to former Fed trader Joseph Wang was created to enable Chinese access to US funding: "The new FIMA Repo Facility is largely a China Repo Facility" (https://fedguy.com/china-repo-facility/; last accessed March 23, 2022).

Table 2 Reserve accumulation, 2000–2022.

2022	BRICS	Brazil	Russia	India	China	SA	US	UK	Euro
FX share % global	38.23	2.71	4.16	4.70	26.14	0.51	0.30	0.92	2.63
FX share as % GDP	17.70	16.91	22.19	16.61	17.49	14.96	0.14	3.58	2.22
2000	BRICS	Brazil	Russia	India	China	SA	US	UK	Euro
FX share % global	2.87	2.18	0.26	0.40	1.79	0.06	2.10	2.30	14.71
FX share as % GDP	7.95	4.95	9.34	7.96	13.67	3.82	0.30	18.75	3.37

Source: *Bloomberg Terminal, World Bank.*

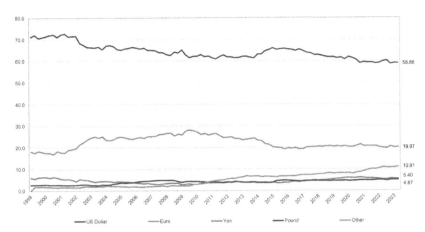

Figure 2 Currency composition of global reserve currencies (1999–2023).
Source: *IMF COFER data.*

15.6 billion).[18] While these changes are comparatively small, they provide a novel form of contestation of the existing GFO resulting from the rise of the BRICS.

The core contestation on the level of <u>international</u> institutions for balance-of-payments issues is about the role of the IMF. With regard to countries with balance-of-payments constraints, the IMF is crucial within the liberal GFO since it combines the provision of liquidity support for countries under duress with a stringent conditionality that promises to restructure these countries along liberal lines. A number of political economy studies have demonstrated the disproportional influence of the US on the likelihood, the size and the conditionality of IMF loans, as well as the pro-cyclical and growth-constraining nature of traditional IMF conditionalities; post-GFC changes were incremental at best (Kring & Gallagher, 2019, 11–14). From the state-capitalist perspective, these conditionalities are highly problematical. Given that the BRICS are unable to substantially modify the IMF's stance due to limited voting rights (despite China's SDR inclusion in 2016), they have developed alternative arrangements for balance-of-payments or short-term liquidity support during crises.

On the one hand, some of the BRICS have strengthened existing multilateral institutions on the regional level. While small regional institutions such as the Latin American Reserve Fund and the Arab Monetary Fund go back until the 1970s, the GFC has given a major boost to these regional initiatives, including

---

[18] www.bloomberg.com/news/articles/2023-05-16/global-central-banks-use-record-amount-of-yuan-from-pboc-swaps.

the establishment of the Eurasian Fund for Stabilization and Development (including Russia) and of the Chiang Mai Initiative Multilateralization Agreement (CMIM; including China). The CMIM is based on the Chiang Mai Initiative (then comprising the ASEAN member states, as well as China, Japan and South Korea) that had been set up after the 1997 Asian financial crisis as a network of bilateral swap arrangements. The CMIM, however, is not only based on a multilateral reserves pool (instead of bilateral swaps) but can even provide more resources to its member countries than the IMF.[19]

On the other hand, the BRICS have developed the more comprehensive CRA in 2014, committing USD 100 billion for mutual support. This is a much smaller amount at disposal than the CMIM (240) and the IMF (653), but it only has to cater for five countries and provides over-proportional access for its smaller members (Cattaneo et al., 2015, 3). Decision-making within the CRA is more balanced than in the IMF, where the US de facto has a veto power on strategic decisions (Würdemann, 2018). Thirty percent of the assistance can be made available without conditionalities; if a member country requires the remaining 70%, it has to conclude a conditionality-based agreement with the IMF. Given the limited size of resources without conditions and the absence of an independent macroeconomic research facility, the CRA is not yet a comprehensive alternative to the IMF; its main contribution as IMF alternative so far is symbolic (Cattaneo et al., 2015; Würdemann, 2018). The guiding principles of the CRA – likely to impose far fewer conditionalities without increasing the chance of recipient governments defaulting on loans – however are in line with a state-capitalist GFO. From the perspective of BRICS governments, providing conditionality-free loans is also an attractive option as it aligns with the norms and rules that have guided the BRICS countries' individual strategies.

2.3 Central Banks and Monetary Policy

How central banks and monetary policy are governed also matters for GFOs. Central banks are crucial institutions in the management of monetary policies imbued with great powers to influence economic policy. In its contemporary liberal form, central banking is supposed to be a technocratic exercise where independent central banks narrowly focus on price stability and inflation targeting. In a state-capitalist setup, however, central banks are accountable to government and have multiple objectives that go beyond a narrow inflation-targeting regime but often include national development objectives.

---

[19] While similar to the CRA the CMIM is partially linked to the IMF, CMIM members have increased the IMF de-linked portion from 20% to 40% between 2010 and 2021, indicating a shift toward more autonomy.

The <u>domestic</u> context for central banks varies significantly. In the US and UK, for instance, central banks are completely independent from political institutions, narrowly focusing on price stability and inflation (2%), although the Fed's mandate also includes promoting maximum employment.[20] In South Africa, the central bank is also independent – even owned by private share-holders – although its mandate slightly diverges from the liberal ideal type through a broader inflating targeting window (3–6%), by acting as a banking regulator, and through managing South Africa's substantial FX reserves. In Brazil, the central bank has recently become independent under the Bolsonaro administration, which pushed forth a liberalization program that included central bank independence since the central bank was part of the Ministry of Finance (MoF) up until 2021 – although this newly won independence is challenged by the Lula government that was elected in 2023.[21] In contrast, while formally independent, Russia's central bank became increasingly politicized under the Putin administration in the early 2000s (Johnson, 2004; Viktorov & Abramov, 2016). Next to inflation targeting, it is also responsible for financial stability, banking regulation and the countries' substantial FX reserves, while it acts on behalf of Russia's MoF. With the tightening of state control over Russia's financial system after 2022, this independence was further compromised. India's central bank is even more dependent with government control also increasing in recent years and a multifaceted mandate that includes inflation control (4%), government debt and cash management, ensuring financial market stability and overseeing current and capital accounts. In China, the central bank is closest to the state-capitalist ideal type that is closely intertwined with national government and a multitude of mandates including inflation targeting (3%) but also facilitating economic growth, maintaining full employment, managing balance of payments, guaranteeing financial stability and maintaining financial reforms.

While South Africa had already moved toward an independent central bank in the 1990s and Brazil more recently adopted such liberal principles, we can observe considerable pushback against the liberal paradigm of "central bank interdependence" from China, India and Russia. While Russia's central bank had been independent during the 1990s, it has become much more politically influenced over time – a process that only intensified after 2022. Similarly, while India's central bank had achieved a degree of independence during the

---

[20] While it is debatable whether Western central banks are apolitical and whether they stretch their mandates (e.g. quantitative easing, other unconventional practices), they remain largely independent from their respective governments.

[21] www.reuters.com/world/americas/brazils-lula-says-he-could-review-central-banks-autonomy-after-end-current-heads-2023-02-03/ (last accessed November 10, 2023).

2000s, in recent years we could observe an increasing politicization of its actions. In China, the government never conceded to central bank interdependence, while it also took on additional political tasks in recent years.[22] In all three countries, the turn toward more authoritarian governance/governments (Putin, Modi, Xi) intensified this development. We can thus observe an increasing resistance on behalf of these countries to conform with liberal norms of monetary governance.

Transnationally, the BRICS' contestation of monetary policies within the liberal GFO increasingly focuses on the promotion of central bank digital currencies (CBDCs). From the BRICS perspective, CBDCs have major advantages. First, they allow cross-border payments that avoid the Western-controlled global payments infrastructure that is based on SWIFT and the network of correspondence banks that focuses on the US financial sector (Nölke, 2022). This would also help to undermine the role of the US dollar as the global trade currency. In the future, CBDCs should be used not only for domestic retail payments by consumers (currently its main purpose) but also for wholesale cross-border trading. An added advantage is a much stronger supervision of payments by (state-controlled) central banks. This would also support the implementation of sophisticated capital controls, given the high degree of state control over this type of digital currencies (Liu & Papa, 2022; Nölke, 2022). More liberal central banks have long been more skeptical of CBDCs, for the same reasons. In India, Russia and especially China, the governments have launched CBDC pilot projects, while Brazil is working on Proof of Concepts. Of all BRICS countries, merely South Africa is still in the initial research phase, just like the UK and the US (Table 3). Correspondingly, more state-capitalist central banks have pressed ahead with the development of CBDCs, while liberal central banks have only reluctantly started initial research. Moreover, there have been considerable attempts by China to facilitate cross-border use of non-Western CBDCs, for instance, with the mBridge project in cooperation with the central banks of Hong Kong, Thailand and the UAE.

In the international dimension, finally, the core issue between a liberal and a state-capitalist GFO is how to manage the global repercussions of the most powerful central bank monetary policies – particularly the US Fed and the European Central Bank (ECB). From a liberal perspective, central banks have a narrow mandate to fight inflation domestically, without concerns about the implications of their policy decisions on other economies (e.g. the Volcker shock). This may also entail major waves of speculative financial flows across

---

[22] A point in case is the revision of China's Central Bank Law in 2020, which now officially includes macro-prudential management next to monetary policy in the central bank mandate.

Table 3 Country involvement with central bank digital currency projects.

Country	Stage	Score
United States	Research	1
United Kingdom	Research	1
South Africa	Research	1
Brazil	Proof of Concept	2
Russia	Pilot	3
India	Pilot	3
China	Pilot	3

Source: *Central Bank Digital Currency Tracker (www.cbdctracker .org; data from November 2023).*

borders. In times of very aggressive monetary policies ("quantitative easing"), many investors invest cheap credits taken up in the advanced economies in emerging economies, leading to overvalued currencies in the latter. In times of a restrictive monetary policy ("taper"), speculative money flows back to the advanced economies, thereby leading to a sudden loss of currency valuation in emerging economies (Bonizzi & Kaltenbrunner, 2018). The governments of countries that have been particularly affected by these wild swings – such as Brazil and India – have repeatedly articulated their critique of the Fed's unilateral decisions (Engel, 2016, 13).

The problematical spillover effects of US monetary policy normalization on the BRICS have been confirmed by several studies (e.g. Ca'Zorzi et al., 2020; Deng et al., 2022; Mohan & Kapur, 2019). Correspondingly, a state-capitalist GFO asks for an international management of monetary policies in order to avoid this type of problems (Rakshit, 2017, 94). This would be in line with the government-controlled model of monetary policy in state capitalism. Whereas central banks in liberal capitalism have no mandate to look after the international repercussions of the monetary decisions, governments of state-capitalist economies might cooperate with other governments and instruct central banks accordingly. The BRICS have, for instance, repeatedly called for enhanced global monetary policy coordination in international fora such as the G20 (Tian, 2016, 119). However, these calls have been in vain. The ECB and the Fed clearly position themselves against formal international policy coordination, except for impromptu coordination in a severe global crisis (Ca'Zorzi et al., 2020; Clarida, 2021). Moreover, given the structural power of major Western central banks – particularly the US Fed – and the internal heterogeneity of the BRICS in terms of central bank independence, the construction of alternative international institutions of monetary policy cooperation that might challenge Western dominance has not yet materialized.

3 Contestation of the Finance Sub-order

While the monetary sub-order matters mostly for macroeconomic issues, the finance sub-order relates to six issue areas that influence the microeconomic level of company financing within GFO. The first two issues link the financing of companies predominantly to the international level. We therefore explore (Section 3.1) short-term portfolio investments and international capital mobility as well as (Section 3.2) more long-term FDI and their governance. We then analyze different dimensions of company finance, starting with (Section 3.3) corporate ownership and governance, before turning to how companies mobilize new funding by investigating (Section 3.4) banks and banking regulations as well as (Section 3.5) financial markets and their regulation. Finally, we analyze (Section 3.6) accounting standards that inform investors about the financial situation of companies. In many of these areas, we can see significant contestation by the BRICS.

3.1 International Capital Mobility

How financial capital moves around the globe is a central feature of global finance. Especially since the 1980s, we can observe an increasing push on abolishing capital controls around the world spearheaded by the US (Helleiner, 1995). Internationally, the removal of capital controls is further enshrined in the OECD Capital Mobility Codex, ideologically defended by the IMF and administered through the methodologies of index providers where private authorities steer financial capital based on their assessment of capital openness. However, allowing the free movement of capital shifts the balance of power between private financial actors and national governments, putting significant pressures on the latter to comply with liberal norms. From a state-capitalist perspective, some degree of capital controls is thus essential for maintaining state capacity.

We can thus observe significant differences in whether countries facilitate capital market openness domestically. The *Chinn–Ito Financial Openness Index* (Chinn and Ito, 2006),[23] for instance, finds that the US, UK and Eurozone have almost perfectly open capital accounts (each with a score of 2.31). While the US has long had an open capital account, we can observe how

---

[23] This widely used measure of financial openness codifies the tabulation of restrictions on cross-border financial transactions reported in the IMF's annual *Exchange Arrangements and Exchange Restrictions* report (IMF, 2021).

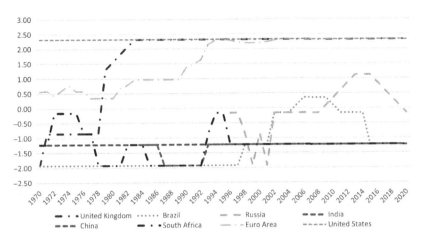

Figure 3 Chinn–Ito Financial Openness Index, 1970–2020.
Source: *Chinn–Ito Index.*

the UK and Europe abolished capital controls during the heyday of neoliberalism in the 1980s and 1990s. In contrast, capital mobility faces many restrictions
in the BRICS. While South Africa experienced brief periods of liberalization in
the 1970s and 1990s, it is today on par with India and China whose capital
accounts still largely remain closed (–1.23). In contrast, Brazil and Russia have
both experienced a more extensive capital liberalization during the 2000s,
although both have been reverting back to a more closed regime over time.
While Brazil changed course during the GFC in 2008 and was almost at the
same level as China, India or South Africa (–1.0), Russia started placing
restrictions on capital controls in 2015 with its index value falling to –0.16 by
2020 (Figure 3).[24] Academic literature paint a similar picture, although empha-
sizing a relatively large degree of capital mobility in Brazil and Russia, followed by South Africa, China's managed opening, and India, which is relatively
closed (Dierckx, 2013; Petry et al., 2021b).

Importantly, US financial actors, both public and private, have been key
drivers in the <u>transnational</u> promotion of international capital mobility and
liberal financial regulations more broadly (Helleiner, 1995). Especially since
the GFC, Anglo-American index providers have emerged as market authorities
that influence countries' financial policies. This is because their decisions to
include countries into their indices that serve as key benchmarks for investors
steer huge financial flows in and out of countries (Fichtner et al., 2022; Cormier
& Naqvi, 2023; Petry et al., 2021a). However, we can observe that the BRICS

---

[24] While no updated data is available at this point, capital account closing has likely increased after
Western sanctions changing Russian financial policies following the Ukraine invasion.

partially resist pressures to conform with these liberal norms. The most powerful index provider MSCI – that, in the words of the *Financial Times*, "in effect
controls the definition of which countries are 'emerging markets'" (Authers,
2018) – has included China, India and Brazil in its watch list of countries that
restrict foreign investment practices, threatening to downgrade them (MSCI,
2018a; Tan & Robertson, 2018).

In 2018, for instance, on behalf of their regulator, India's stock exchanges
terminated market data agreements with MSCI after increasing fears about
losing control over domestic capital markets as derivatives businesses moved
to the Singapore Exchange (SGX) where Nifty index futures (India's equivalent
of the S&P500) were traded. Despite significant pressures from MSCI, which
effectively threatened India with index exclusion, a subsequent loss of status as
well as investment outflows (MSCI, 2018b), India managed to maintain its
index weighting and essentially forced SGX to form a joint venture with the
National Stock Exchange (NSE) of India (NSE IFSC-SGX Connect) and route
its trades through GIFT City, India's new international financial center.[25]
Ultimately, this setup maintains India with a lever of state-capitalist control
over capital inflows.

Arguably, China follows the state-capitalist ideal type even more closely by
strictly regulating, monitoring and intervening into the activities of foreign
investors, creating sophisticated investment channels that allow the trading of
Chinese securities while maintaining capital controls and maintaining state
control over market infrastructures (Petry, 2021b). However, despite China
retaining the state-capitalist features of its financial system while strategically
opening up its capital account, global investors have been reallocating money to
China (Lockett & Hale, 2020). This is largely due to China's inclusion into
global benchmark indices, which acted as a catalyst that propelled evermore
investment into Chinese markets and are assumed to have steered at least
USD180 billion of passive and active investments into China's stock market
by May 2021. Essentially, the decision of global index providers to include
China in its global benchmark indices legitimized China's non-liberal rules of
how markets operate, actively supporting state-capitalist market organization
practices, both financially and normatively. In contrast, the other BRICS seem
to more readily comply with the standards set out by index providers, where
only Brazil has a few minor issues with foreign investor accessibility, while
South Africa mostly complies with liberal principles (MSCI, 2021, 2023). Until
2022, Russia had also mostly complied with liberal norms but has since

---

[25] www.livemint.com/market/stock-market-news/sgx-nifty-to-get-delisted-nse-ifsc-sgx-connect-
to-become-operational-read-here-11681894066636.html.

dramatically changed course. Foreign investors from "unfriendly countries" (that have imposed sanctions after its invasion of Ukraine) are no longer able to trade Russian securities; as a result, MSCI discontinued all Russian indices. The BRICS are partially resisting pressures to conform with liberal norms of capital openness, which Anglo-American financial actors are trying to enforce.

With respect to the <u>international</u> level, the IMF stands out as an important institution for the enforcement of capital movement liberalization (Chwieroth, 2010).[26] Traditionally, capital account liberalization was a core conditionality demanded in the context of IMF SAPs, which most BRICS countries underwent at some point (Section 4.1). For a state-capitalist GFO, this is a key cornerstone of contention since it intrusively disrupts national sovereignty (see Section 1). In this context, it is important to note that the IMF has substantially revised its strong position on capital controls in recent years. While the IMF for a long time advocated for capital controls, a 2012 background paper (IMF, 2012) indicated that empirical evidence for capital flow regulation is mixed, a substantial modification of the core principle of the GFO. This is partially due to resistance from countries like the BRICS.

Importantly, the BRICS, especially China, India and Brazil, have been vocal critics of the IMF's approach to capital controls, advocating for a review of its policy position (Dierckx, 2013; Dierckx, 2015). On the one hand, the BRICS put external pressure on the IMF through noncompliance by implementing (Brazil) or maintaining (India and China) capital controls and by repeatedly publicly criticizing the IMF's policy position, especially by India and Brazil (Bretton Woods Project, 2011), while South Africa and Russia had been less vocal on this issue. On the other hand, the BRICS used their growing power within the IMF since more of their people were appointed to important positions. Paulo Nogueira Batista, then executive director who represented Brazil on the IMF Board, for instance, criticizes its "pro-liberalization" bias (Beattie, 2012), while Zhu Min, who had been appointed as the IMF's deputy managing director, urged for recognition of the differential needs of emerging and developing economies with respect to the IMF's for capital mobility framework (Gruin et al., 2018). As Derek Scissors, an expert on Asia economic policy at the Heritage Foundation noted, "Zhu's appointment and the perception shift over capital controls were all part of a broader change within the IMF" (Parameswaran, 2010). In addition, the BRICS formed a coalition with a unified voice at the IMF Executive Board, voicing their criticism of liberal capital flow rules. Through these measures, as Gallagher (2015, 24) noted,

---

[26] While the OECD operates a comprehensive set of regulations/ reports (e.g. "OECD Codes of Liberalization of Capital Movements"; OECD, 2021), it has no power to enforce these regulations.

"the BRICS nations were [ultimately] able to exercise power as autonomy by protecting their ability to exercise cooperative decentralization to regulate capital flows." Overall, we can therefore assess a certain degree of international contestation from (parts of) the BRICS when it comes to the issue of capital mobility.

3.2 Foreign Direct Investment

How productive capital moves around the global economy is another crucial dimension of GFOs. Similar to the free flow of financial capital (portfolio investment), the liberal perspective propagates the abolishment of national restrictions on FDI to enable commercially oriented activities. Deep liberalization is thereby further facilitated through multilateral investment treaties/ BITs, while private companies have a strong position vis-à-vis national governments via arbitration panels (Dafe & Williams, 2021). In contrast, state-capitalist logic emphasizes the need to restrict inward FDI (IFDI) flows based on strategic considerations, for example, only opening certain economic sectors or facilitating technology/knowledge transfers through joint venture requirements. While partially commercial outward FDI (OFDI) flows are often strategically oriented or embedded in specific industrial strategies, their investment treaties put limits on liberalization, and arbitration panels are not important since they would impede state capacity.

We can thus observe significant variation when it comes to the <u>domestic</u> dimension of IFDI. For this, we utilize the OECD's *FDI Regulatory Restrictiveness Index*, which calculates a metric based on foreign equity limitations, screening/approval mechanisms, restrictions on employing foreign key personnel and other operational restrictions. From this data, we can observe that FDI restrictions are lowest in the UK (0.04), followed by South Africa (0.06), Brazil (0.08) and the US (0.09). Brazil and South Africa have significantly liberalized their IFDI regimes in recent years and are on par with liberal market economies; it is also noteworthy that the US is more restrictive than the OECD average (0.06), albeit still in the liberal spectrum. In contrast, despite a process of global liberalization efforts (see "Average") over the last twenty years that encompassed all countries (Figure 4), India (0.21), China (0.22) and Russia (0.26) firmly remain on the state-capitalist spectrum especially utilizing investment approval/screenings as well as restrictions on ownership (and hiring foreign management in the case of China).[27] Thereby, Russia, India and China retain some of the most restrictive FDI regulations globally (Figure 5). Rather than

---

[27] In all three countries, this is supplemented by other restrictions like needing to form joint ventures with local companies to ensure technology and skill transfers (Beausang, 2012, 29, 34, 45).

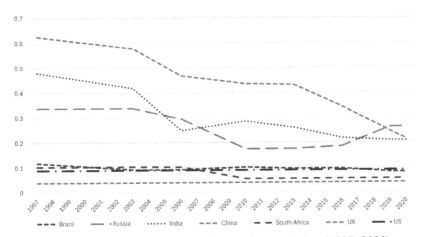

Figure 4 OECD FDI Regulatory Restrictiveness Index (1997–2020).

Source: *OECD.Stat.*

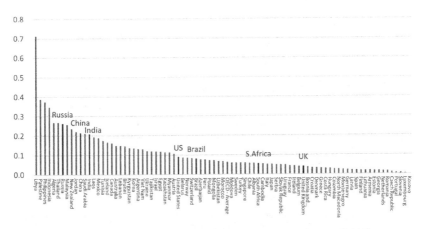

Figure 5 OECD FDI Regulatory Restrictiveness Index (2020).

Source: *OECD.Stat.*

encompassing liberalization, they have only selectively opened their countries to foreign investment, protecting strategically important sectors, limiting foreign ownership and facilitating knowledge transfers in order to boost national economic development. We can thus observe considerable contestation of the liberal FDI regime at the domestic level in some of the BRICS.

These differences in FDI regimes also extend beyond the domestic into the transnational sphere. When it comes to such OFDI flows, the BRICS have also become much more important, increasing their share of global OFDI from 0.61% in 2000 to an astonishing 20.1% by 2020 having long overtaken the UK and almost on par with the US in terms of their share of global OFDI flows

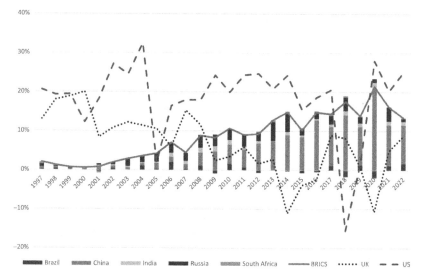

Figure 6 OFDI flows (1990–2022).

Source: *UNCTAD.*

(Figure 6). The majority of this development can be attributed to the internationalization of Chinese companies, which accounted for 70% of BRICS-OFDI and OFDIs from Russia, which accounted for another 20%, while India, South Africa and Brazil only account for a small part of this development (De Conti & Diegues, 2022). Importantly, these Chinese OFDI flows differ substantially from OFDIs from the US or UK.

While Chinese companies (both private and state-owned enterprises (SOEs)) have evolved into profit-oriented entities, their actions are informed by both commercial and state objectives. This internationalization of Chinese companies was partially initiated by the state ("going global" strategy) and is influenced by state objectives like "Made in China 2025" or the need to secure access to strategically important resources (ten Brink, 2015; Jiang, 2009). While there is no official internationalization strategy, the international expansion of Russian firms is based on a combination of economic and political factors, with the state playing a strong role in promoting OFDI and strongly supporting the foreign subsidiaries of Russian SOEs (Holtbrügge & Kreppel, 2012, 17). India also does not have an official OFDI policy. Albeit limited in scope, the aim of Indian OFDI has often been access to resources and technology and was often accomplished by establishing joint ventures with foreign partners. In Brazil, there is also no official policy, but the Brazilian Development Bank (BNDES) offers below-market interest rates to select companies and OFDI was incentivized via tax-cuts. In South Africa, the state encourages investment into other African countries but without any formal regulatory policy. Generally, government support for OFDIs is much stronger in China and Russia – especially in industries that have been declared as strategic such as oil and gas industries in Russia or the automobile and electronic industries in China (Holtbrügge & Kreppel, 2012) – while the internationalization of Brazilian, Indian and South African firms is less pronounced and more market-driven.

Importantly, FDIs are not regulated by an intergovernmental institution. The negotiation of a "Multilateral Agreement on Investments" failed some decades ago. The United Nations Conference on Trade and Development (UNCTAD) keeps track of FDI flows and provides recommendations but does not have any formal authority. However, over time, an international "regime" to govern international investment (Simmons, 2014) has emerged, which now forms a core part of the liberal GFO: investor–state dispute settlement (ISDS). While by 2000 there had been only 44 arbitration cases, by 2023 UNCTAD's *Investment Dispute Settlement Navigator* reported a total of 1,257 cases. In this regime, private arbitration panels negotiate the claims of international investors against host governments. Importantly, ISDS thereby often works in favor of foreign investors as ISDS effectively gives firms the same rights as countries and the overall regime is geared toward maintaining free movement of capital (Weghmann & Hall, 2021). There is, for instance, no scope for a review through national courts even if private rulings violate domestic public policy. As this mainly benefits Western MNCs, it is not surprising that 70% of all ISDS claims that have been filed are from the US and European MNCs (Gray, 2020). From a state-capitalist perspective, ISDS is therefore highly problematic, since it is based on a "dubious" form of private regulation and works against state sovereignty.

Correspondingly, we see major differences with regard to ISDS (Table 4): Whereas ISDS is regularly included in BITs by Western states, several BRICS states rather avoid or withdraw from this type of institution (Samples, 2019, 146–147). India, Brazil and South Africa thereby contest this regime the most. In contrast to China and Russia, neither of these countries has, for instance, signed the *World Bank's International Centre for Settlement of Investment Disputes* (ICSID), the leading body that provides the framework for the conduct of arbitration proceedings.[28] As Julia Gray (2020, 11–17) demonstrates, Brazil and South Africa have even opted to pull back from investment treaties that open them up to international arbitration. Brazil was never a part of the global web of BITs and has established its own "Cooperation and Facilitation Investment Agreement" framework that "focuses on the promotion and facilitation of investment, rather than on investors' protection" and state-to-state arbitration rather than investor–state

---

[28] ICSID has been signed by 165 member states; Brazil, India and South Africa are the only G20 members that have not signed the convention (https://icsid.worldbank.org/sites/default/files/ICSID%203/ICSID-3–ENG.pdf).

Table 4 Bilateral investment treaties (BITs) by country (2023).

	Brazil	India	South Africa	Russia	China	UK	US
Terminated	0	76	12	5	22	14	2
In force	2	8	12	64	106	85	39

Source: *UNCTAD International Investment Agreements Navigator.*

arbitration (Potin & Brito de Urquiza, 2021; Moraes & Hees, 2018). Meanwhile, South Africa decided to exit many BITs after an existing arbitration case (Foresti vs. South Africa) threatened to disrupt domestic public policies concerning environmental preservation and Black Economic Empowerment (Ranjan et al., 2018, 10). India, in contrast, "wants to be a part of the system although with different terms of engagement" (Ranjan et al., 2018). It therefore unilaterally terminated all of its existing BITs with mostly developed countries, asked for "joint interpretive statements to clarify ambiguities" as well as "avoid expansive interpretations by arbitration tribunals" and built up a network of BITs based on its own "India Model BIT 2015" framework that retains a greater degree of state sovereignty.

In contrast to these actions, Russia and China in contrast have large BIT networks and are deeply integrated into the ISDS system, similar to the US and UK. China has the second largest number of BITs globally (106), while Russia (64) signed more BITs than the US (39). Given that especially China and, to a lesser degree, Russia are large providers of OFDI, their own companies potentially benefit from these treaties, and we can see them increasingly becoming claimants as well. However, both states simultaneously try to shield themselves against too much disruption of their state power (Gray, 2020, 10). As Huiping Chen (2019) notes, China's embrace of ISDS should be understood as a way to protect China's outbound investors, to shape the global ISDS regime and to offer alternative Chinese-initiated international institutions in order to disrupt the current monopoly of Western institutions.

Overall, the liberal FDI regime is quite substantially contested by the BRICS. From restrictions on IFDIs, to state-capitalist OFDIs and the ISDS regime, we can observe substantial contestation of the international investment regime from different BRICS countries.

3.3 Corporate Ownership and Governance

Another important component of GFOs is who owns corporations and how this translates into their governance. The liberal perspective advocates a free market for corporate control (high "free-float" of shares) and corporate ownership

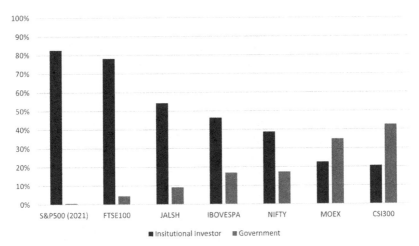

Figure 7 Corporate ownership patterns (aggregate; 2023).
Source: *Bloomberg Terminal, company websites.*

through institutional investors, which seek to maximize their profits on behalf of their shareholders and thus incentivized corporations to make their businesses efficient and profitable (Lazonick & O'Sullivan, 2000). This differs significantly under state capitalism. While albeit utilizing market mechanisms for economic allocation – which includes the listing of (state-owned) companies – state-capitalist economies maintain a significant degree of state ownership in listed companies while at the same time limiting the influence and ownership of foreign institutional investors.

To compare corporate ownership patterns between the BRICS, US and UK, we analyzed stock ownership data from 1,413 companies listed on <u>domestic</u> stock markets.[29] We can thereby observe significant variations (Figure 7). The US and UK are closest to the liberal ideal types with very high ownership by institutional investors (78–83%),[30] while state ownership is very small (0.6–4.6%). Brazil and South Africa are mixed cases, with relatively high degrees of institutional ownership (46–54%) as well as moderate levels of state ownership (9–17%). In contrast, Russia and India are much more state-capitalist with lower levels of institutional ownership (22–39%) and significant state ownership (17–35%). China is even

---

[29] Our sample includes Bloomberg terminal data on all companies of the respective countries' benchmark stock index: Brazil (IBOVESPA), Russia (MOEX), India (Nifty), China (CSI300), South Africa (JALSH), UK (FTSE100) and US (S&P500); importantly, across ownership data is often patchy, so a 5% error margin should be factored in.

[30] "Institutional investor" ownership is defined as the sum of the following ownership categories displayed on the Bloomberg Terminal: investment advisor, venture capital, private equity, pension fund, mutual fund, endowment, insurance company and hedge fund.

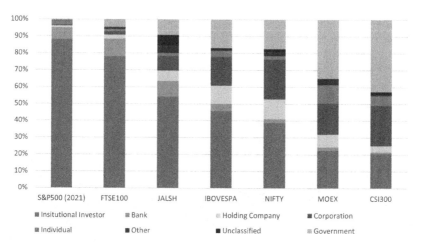

Figure 8 Corporate ownership patterns (disaggregated; 2023).
Source: *Bloomberg Terminal, company websites.*

closer to the state-capitalist ideal type, with state ownership (43%) even exceeding institutional ownership (21%).

Importantly, state influence on corporate governance also manifests through different channels, which makes state influence probably even more prevalent in state-capitalist economies.[31] First, state ownership might be hidden through different layers of investment structures. Second, some types of ownership are more susceptible to state influence than others (Figure 8). In China, Russia, India and Brazil, next to the government, holding companies (4–12%), corporations (17–24%) and individuals (2–11%) own significant company shares. For instance, SOEs often hold shares in other corporations, either directly or via holding companies. Further, influencing individual owners (e.g. Russian oligarchs, Chinese party members, Indian business families) is much easier than influencing foreign asset managers or hedge funds, especially in economic systems where socioeconomic ties between political and business elites are crucial coordination mechanisms (Nölke et al., 2020). Third, other measures of state influence on companies can exist. In China, for instance, the authorities have also been promoting the presence and power of "party organizations" (*dang zuzhi*) to boost private sector compliance with government priorities.[32]

This also has <u>transnational</u> implications. From a state-capitalist perspective, foreign ownership – especially from Anglo-American institutional investors – should be curtailed since these might evade state control and impede national

---

[31] Other estimates of South Africa's ownership distribution indicate a similar pattern to Brazil (OECD, 2019).

[32] Source: https://macropolo.org/party-committees-private-sector-china/?rp=m.

development policies. While foreign ownership is, for instance, very high in the UK (74.82%),[33] it is somewhat lower in South Africa (52%) and Brazil (43%) and significantly lower in Russia (25%), India (20%) and China (5%) (Petry et al., 2021b). In China, for instance, individual foreign owners cannot hold more than 10% of a companies' stock while the total limit of foreign company ownership is 30%. Investments in India's stock market had been similarly regulated, with foreigners only allowed to hold 10–49% of many listed companies (although restrictions were relaxed in April 2020). In Russia, historically, foreigners could only own 25–50% of strategically important companies active in media, banking, infrastructures (e.g. railways, pipelines, electricity, telecommunications), commodities (e.g. mining, oil/gas) or with military ties (e.g. weapons, aviation, encryption); given the structure of Russia's economy, this included the majority of its investible companies. In addition, from September 2023 onwards, a new law came into effect where investors from "unfriendly states" risk having their assets seized and given to their Russian co-owners (Braw, 2023). Similar to Russia's historical approach, sectoral restrictions also exist in South Africa, albeit with higher investment limits, whereas investment into Brazilian companies is relatively liberalized with only a few restrictions on banking, mining, telecommunication, media and healthcare.

Reversely, we can observe an increasing transnationalization of state-led investment practices (Babic et al., 2020). First, we see clear differences between senders and recipients of transnational state-capitalist investment. While China and Russia are exporting large amounts of state capital, Brazil, South Africa and India are doing this to a lesser extent (India is rather a recipient of state-capitalist investment). Similarly, there is very little state-capitalist investment from the US and UK both being rather large recipients of this type of capital. Second, there are considerable differences between the characteristics of state-capitalist investment. What little state-capital the US invested abroad is in the form of portfolio investment, which is also a significant portion of state-capitalist investment from South Africa and the UK. In contrast, investment coming from Brazil, Russia, China and India is mostly in the form of majority stakes (Figure 9). Rather than financial portfolio investment aiming to maximize shareholder value, state-led transnational investment from the BRICs is aimed at controlling target companies. It is thus very likely that rather than impatient capital as portrayed by liberal institutional investors, this state-led investment represents an important source of patient capital that is based on long-term strategies aimed at national development objectives (Kaplan, 2021).

---

[33] While US foreign ownership is only 21.32%, this number is misleading since "foreign investors" are usually US-based institutions.

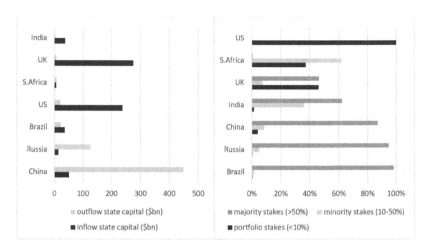

Figure 9 Transnational state capital flows (a) and investment strategies (b).
Source: *Data from Babic et al. (2020); authors' calculation.*

State ownership of corporations is not comprehensively regulated on the
international level; this is mostly left to national governments. However, one
partial exception is the regulation of SWFs, state-owned investment funds that
pursue a mix of commercially oriented and policy/strategically oriented investments (Liu & Dixon, 2021). Here, a fairly comprehensive regulation is in the
interest of the liberal GFO, since its proponents are worried that SWFs give
foreign governments a too strong hold over private companies. In contrast, from
a state-capitalist perspective, SWFs are fully legitimate and useful instruments
as they can facilitate national development policies. Especially since the GFC,
SWFs have become much more powerful financial actors globally with their
assets under management increasing from less than USD1 trillion in 2000 to
USD11.9 trillion in 2023 (SWFI, 2023).[34]

Nonetheless, international regulation of SWFs remains quite limited, pos-
sibly indicating a weakening of the liberal GFO. The G7 had, for instance, asked
the IMF to create a code of conduct for SWF regulation. Against initial opposition by Russia and notably China, an international working group convened by
the IMF in 2008 succeeded with negotiating a code that was then also accepted
by China, the so-called "Generally Accepted Principles and Practices/GAPP" or
"Santiago Principles" (Sohn, 2013, 641). The Santiago Principles signatures
correspondingly formed the International Forum of Sovereign Wealth Funds

---

[34] Next to Norway and Asia, most SWF assets are concentrated among existing BRICS members –
especially China, but also Russia – and new BRICS members like Saudi Arabia, Dubai, Abu
Dhabi and Iran.

(IFSWF) as a voluntary organization with the aim of "strengthening the [SWF] community through dialogue, research and self-assessment."[35] However, an in-depth study of the implementation of the code concludes that the Santiago Principles are "absolutely futile for considering and protecting the interests of the host states of sovereign investments" (Bismuth, 2017, 69). The scope of the "Santiago Principles" is very limited, they are voluntarily endorsed by IFSWF members (including China, India and Russia), their performance is self-assessed in an intransparent way in the absence of independent monitoring and enforcement, compliance has been "underwhelming" and the forum itself is subject to limited transparency, accountability and governance (Chijioke-Oforji, 2019). Officially, the matter is regulated according to liberal economic principles. Its implementation, however, works against the latter and in favor of SWFs, a core instrument of state capitalism. Overall, we can thus observe considerable contestation of corporate ownership issues across countries and levels of analysis.

3.4 Commercial Banks and Banking Regulations

Another important dimension of GFOs is how and by whom credit is allocated, a process where banks and their regulation play a crucial role. Following a liberal logic, banks should be privately owned and operated in order to facilitate profit-driven lending activity. Banking is thus partially self-regulated (e.g. utilization of credit ranking, bank's own risk calculation systems), which should also inform a singular, harmonized global system of banking regulation as with the Basel Committee on Banking Supervision (BCBS). In contrast, a certain degree of state influence/control over the allocation of credit is crucial in a state-capitalist economy. Consequently, banks are therefore much more likely to be partially state-owned/controlled in order to facilitate policy-driven lending activity. These state-owned banks (SOBs) control a significant part of banking assets, while bank regulation is much more state-centered and in line with national policy priorities.

We can thus observe significant variation when it comes to <u>domestic</u> banking systems (Figure 10). We therefore analyzed the share of SOBs as well as foreign banks with respect to total banking assets. Here, we see a clear picture with (very) high volumes of state-directed lending in Russia (72%), India (70%), China (51%) as well as Brazil (41%). In contrast, SOBs only play a small role in South Africa (4%) and are largely absent in the US and UK (if not counting nationalized banks).[36]

---

[35] www.ifswf.org/about-us.
[36] State-ownership for UK due to nationalization of failed banks (RBS, NatWest and Lloyds).

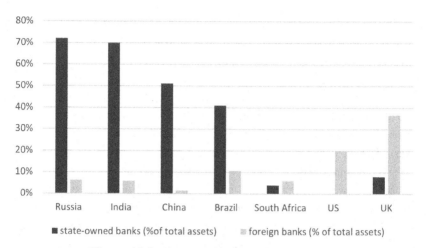

Figure 10 State ownership in banking systems.

Source: *Bloomberg Terminal, Statista, financial news.*

Interestingly, we can observe reversed trends over time in the BRICS. In China and India, we see a slow decline of SOBs as SOB assets accounted for 72% in 2003 (Vernikov, 2015) and 69.9% in 2008 (RBI, 2013), respectively. In both countries, a moderate degree of private competition was allowed to mobilize more funds for industrial development as too much state involvement created inefficiencies in credit allocation. In contrast, both Russia and Brazil witnessed a strengthening of SOBs after privatization experiments during the 1990s. In Russia, the SOB share of bank assets stood at only 35% in 2000 (Vernikov, 2017), while the Brazilian share of public-bank assets increased from 29.4% in 2002 (Wolters et al., 2014). While – similar to the UK and US – the share of SOBs in South Africa has been historically quite low, we can observe the formation of a more robust form of state-owned banking in Russia, India, China and, to a lesser degree, Brazil that combines a (moderately) high degree of state ownership with some private banking activity, although this new form of state-owned banking is not reliant on foreign banks.

Importantly, this new constellation also has implications for <u>transnational</u> lending patterns. Since the 1980s, profit-driven Western banks have internationalized and emerged as important global players. But while foreign banks accounted for 12.4% of banking assets in the US, 36.6% in the UK (2019) and 12.2% across the European Union (EBA, 2022),[37] they have only made unequal inroads in the BRICS. In Brazil, foreign banks account for 10.7% of banking assets, less so in South Africa (6.0%), India (5.9%) and Russia (6.3%),

---

[37] Importantly, this figure only applies to non-EU banks, not EU banks from other countries.

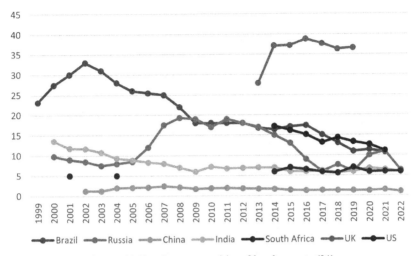

Figure 11 Foreign ownership of bank assets (%).

Source: *Various policy reports (IMF, central banks) and financial news.*

and with an even smaller footprint in China (1.0%) (Figure 11). While both Brazil and Russia experimented with banking sector liberalization in the 1990s and 2000s, foreign banks actually became less important over time in an effort to regain control over their liberalized banking systems. In South Africa and India, the share of foreign banks remained at a relatively stable low level, while in China the small share of foreign banks has decreased even further in recent years. This is because from a state-capitalist perspective, foreign bank ownership impedes the state's ability to influence credit allocation.

In addition to such resistance to conform with liberal rules, we can observe an increasing transnationalization of SOBs from the BRICS. Importantly, this lending has different characteristics than that of Western banks (Table 5). By mid-2018, Chinese banks have become the fifth largest global creditors, accounting for 7.1% of outstanding cross-border lending, with US banks accounting for 11.3% and UK banks for 9.5% (Cerutti et al., 2020, 24). But while only accounting for 2.4% of credit from advanced economy borrowers – compared to 11.1% (US) and 10.4% (UK) – Chinese banks accounted for 23.7% of lending to developing countries and were the top creditor in sixty-three countries, with a significantly smaller role of US (7.1%) and UK (7.8%). While considerably smaller, the other BRICS also account for 4.5% of lending to developing countries in contrast to 1.5% for advanced economies. When calculating the ratio between lending to advanced and developing economies, it becomes clear that except Russia (0.78), the other BRICS prefer lending to developing rather than advanced economies (0.10–0.31), while Anglo-American banks prefer lending to advanced countries

Table 5 Cross-border lending to advanced and developing economies.

	Brazil	Russia	India	China	S. Africa	US	UK
AEs lending (global %)	0.3	0.7	0.4	2.4	0.2	11.1	10.4
DEs lending (global %)	1.7	0.9	1.3	23.7	0.6	7.1	7.8
Top lender (#)	0	2	1	63	4	9	5
AE–DE ratio	0.17	0.78	0.31	0.10	0.33	1.56	1.34
Portfolio investment DEs (global %)	0	0.1	0	0.4	0.1	35.4	6.5

Source: *Authors' table; data from Cerutti et al. (2020, 36–39).*

(1.34–1.56). Western banks' interactions with developing economies also rather focus on short-term portfolio investment (Cerutti et al., 2020, 26). Overall, lending from BRICS banks – that are, to a large part, state-owned and therefore engage in different lending practices – closes a gap in the global banking system since developing countries were often left out by profit-driven Western banks and now have a BRICS alternative that does not expose them to global financial market pressures (Kaplan, 2021).

On the <u>international</u> level, commercial banking is regulated by the Basel Committee on Banking Supervision ("Basel Committee"). The last major regulation (Basel III) has been issued in 2010, and the previous ones in 1988 (Basel I) and 2007 (Basel II). Importantly, as Woods (2010, 9) noted, "Members of the Basel Committee . . . reflected that the presence of China, India, and Brazil in the G20 has decreased back-sliding which might have occurred as some G7 members encountered opposition to regulation by their powerful global financial sectors." The BRICS have been formally supportive of the Basel process (Larionova & Shelepov, 2022, 521–522) and China was even one of the first countries to incorporate the Basel III agreement into national law. India also implemented Basel regulations very quickly (Jones, 2022, 80), similar to Brazil, which was attested a higher degree of Basel III compliance than the EU and the US during the 2010s (Schapiro, 2024). However, this formal endorsement does not necessarily indicate comprehensive implementation on the ground. China, for instance, very selectively chooses which parts of global banking rules fit well with domestic priorities (Sohn, 2013, 642) and Brazil was able to combine Basel implementation with the requirements of its developmental state (Schapiro, 2024).

Starting with the Basel II process, BRICS member states also have tried to influence the design of global banking rules to make it more compatible with their own requirements. The main issue at stake is the important role of private self-regulation in the Basel II/III regime. Instead of relying on supervision through public regulators (as in Basel I), Basel II gave banks the opportunity of private self-regulation by relying on internal ratings based on market price–based risk assessments, which sits uneasily with state-capitalist prerogatives in China and other BRICS economies (Sohn, 2013, 642–643). Crucially, this provided more sophisticated international banks a competitive advantage over banks in emerging markets:

> Commenting on the 2001 second consultative paper, the Reserve Bank of India complained that, by failing to qualify for internal ratings, emerging market banks would experience a "significant increase" in capital charges. The People's Bank of China, meanwhile, suggested that the proposals "basically address the needs of large and complex banks in G10 countries". Similar worries were articulated by the Banking Council of South Africa . . . .

(Lall, 2010, 22) This opposition did not succeed, due to the advanced state of the negotiation process.

However, a somewhat broader perspective demonstrates an explicit state-capitalist challenge of a core pillar of global banking regulation. The BRICS grouping is deeply unhappy with the existing state of private self-regulation by rating agencies, an important ingredient in Basel II/III banking regulation. The dominant role of the "Big Three" rating agencies – Moody's, Standard & Poor's and Fitch – negatively affect the conditions for sovereign borrowing of the BRICS economies; for example, India (Helleiner & Wang, 2018, 581–583). This also has repercussions on corporate bond issuers and increases their financial costs. Correspondingly, various BRICS policymakers – particularly from India and Russia – have proposed to set up a BRICS credit rating agency. So far, these proposals have not yet led to any tangible result, on the one side due to the structural power of the "Big Three" and on the other side due to the existence of a fairly successful Chinese rating agency (Dagong) with ambitions for transnational expansion (Helleiner & Wang, 2018, 583–589). However, the topic is still on the agenda, as indicated by the meeting of the "BRICS Credit Rating Cooperation Workshop" in October 2022 (Xueqing, 2022). While not very comprehensive and limited in scope, we can still observe a nascent challenge of international banking regulation. Overall, when it comes to banking, a mixed picture emerges with respect to the BRICS challenge, with considerable contestation domestically, an increasing transnational challenge and rather limited international contestation.

3.5 Financial Markets

Financial markets for securities such as stocks or derivatives are another key aspect of GFOs. A crucial dimension here is the governance and ownership of these markets. How financial markets are governed, by whom they are owned, and which constraints and incentives market organizers such as exchanges face influence the kinds of markets that they create. In liberal markets, exchanges are profit-oriented corporations mostly owned by international investors, subject to fierce competition with lots of off-exchange activity, and with a mandate to generate profit. By contrast, in the state-capitalist ideal type, exchanges are (partially) state-oriented entities, less profit-oriented, and foreign ownership of exchanges is restricted.

We can thus observe considerable variation in <u>domestic</u> market setups (Table 6). In China, for instance, exchanges are fully state-owned. For Russia's Moscow Exchange (MOEX) and the NSE of India, state institutions (central bank, NatDBs, etc.) are the largest single shareholders (jointly holding

Table 6 Institutional structures of exchange markets.

	Brazil	Russia	India	China	S. Africa	US	UK
Ownership structure of exchanges	Listed; 0.1% state ownership	Listed; 30.2% state	Listed; NSE – 22.7%, BSE – 14.9% state	Fully state-owned; 100% state	Listed; 13.3% state	Listed; 0% state	Listed; 0% state
Foreign ownership of exchanges (restrictions)	Very extensive; 84.3% (no limit)	Extensive; 55% (only free-float)	Limited; BSE – 7.9%, NSE – 38.1% (max. 49%)	None (not allowed)	Extensive; 37.98% (no limit)	Extensive; ICE/NYSE 32.2%, Nasdaq 45.9% (no limit)	Very extensive; 81.72% (no limit)
Competition from other trading platforms	No; ATS launch sabotaged by B3	Limited; low trading volume	No; ATS forbidden	No; strictly regulated	Limited; JSE owns only ATS	Extensive; market fragmented: eighty-eight trading venues, (NYSE 25%, Nasdaq 11%)	Extensive; market fragmented: thirteen trading venues, plus seventy-three SIs; (LSE 55%)

Source: *Authors' table; adapted from Petry et al. (2021b).*

between 23% and 30%) and only around half of the shares are in free-float and can be publicly traded. Consequently, foreign institutional investor owners hold 38.12% (NSE) and 7.9% (BSE) in India but 55% in Russia, although no foreign shareholder owns more than 6% of outstanding shares. In Russia and India, foreign ownership is capped to prevent foreign control, and state institutions have substantial ownership stakes. In contrast, state ownership in South Africa (13.3%) and Brazil (0.14%) is much smaller/nonexistent, whereas foreign ownership is extensive in Brazil (84.3%) but more moderate in South Africa (38.0%), respectively. In the UK and US, there is no state ownership of stock exchanges, while foreign ownership is 81.72% and 39.1%,[38] respectively.

Resulting from such different ownership structures, exchanges in state-capitalist markets also occupy different positions within national financial systems. While liberal exchanges are subject to market pressures themselves, state-capitalist exchanges are shielded from external competitors while internal competition from other trading platforms is often limited. Off-exchange trans-actions (alternative trading systems/ATS, dark pools, etc.) are largely prohibited in state-capitalist markets, concentrating trading activity within one/few cen-tralized exchange(s), whereas liberal markets are increasingly fragmented (Mattli, 2019). In fact, off-exchange trading is prohibited by law in China or India, while in South Africa the only dark pool is owned by the Johannesburg Stock Exchange (JSE) itself and off-exchange trading in Russia is nonexistent (Petry et al., 2021b). In contrast, US and UK equity markets are highly frag-mented. In the US, for instance, NYSE and Nasdaq account for less than 40% of trading volume and competes with eighty-eight trading venues (Nasdaq, 2021). The London Stock Exchange (LSE) also only accounts for 55% of trading volume, competing with at least twelve other trading platforms. Instead of market players competing in a marketplace for marketplaces, stock exchanges in state-capitalist settings have considerable authority as well as more power over and within their markets.

Next to stock markets, this also extends to the organization of derivative markets, including the extent of over-the-counter (OTC) derivatives trading. Following a liberal logic, the OTC derivatives market creates huge profit opportunities, offers market-based solutions for financial actors and is largely based on transnational industry standards and comparatively light regulation. It is therefore unsurprising that OTC derivative trading has experienced enormous growth in Western markets, with the City of London and Wall Street emerging as global trading hubs. But such unrestricted, opaque markets for leveraged, speculative products are incompatible with a state-capitalist logic of market

---

[38] Average: ICE/NYSE: 32.2%; Nasdaq: 48.9% (Source: Bloomberg Terminal).

organization. As against OTC markets, regulated marketplaces such as exchanges enable a certain degree of control over market activities, for instance, through the introduction of position limits, hedging quotas or monitoring systems (Petry, 2020). Consequently, instead of transnational OTC markets, derivative trading in the BRICS is rather conducted in their respective national exchanges. While it is difficult to compile country-level data on OTC derivative trading for the BRICS, the following comparison might be useful. In 2019, emerging markets as a whole – BRICS and other developing countries – accounted for only 9% of global OTC derivatives trading, the remaining 91% being mostly traded in New York and London (BIS, 2019). In contrast, the BRICS accounted for 56.76% of exchange-traded derivative turnover, with India, Brazil and China emerging as the world's first, third and fourth largest exchange-traded derivatives markets globally.[39] While the BRICS are increasingly financializing, this process is informed by a need to maintain a degree of state control over financial markets.

Another important area of contestation is the transnational spread of profit-oriented market practices such as high frequency trading (HFT). Essentially, HFT represents liberal norms on steroids – market activity that is purely directed to generate profit in a synchronic manner and largely detached from fundamental assessments or long-term perspectives. To enable this type of activity, market infrastructures are crucial. As MacKenzie et al. (2012, 285) noted, in Western capital markets, "a symbiotic relationship" between exchanges and HFT has emerged, as exchanges "provide the infrastructure that makes [HFT] possible" – by enabling colocation, direct market access (DMA), trading speed, multiple order types or order cancellations; in US equity markets, for instance, HFT accounts for 50% of overall trading.

However, such purely profit-oriented market activity goes against state-capitalist logic where more strategic, long-term considerations about national champions or national sovereignty are prioritized purposes of market organization. In China, HFT is consequently very restricted. As Petry (2020, 220–221) demonstrates, the state-owned exchanges deliberately slow down data speed, implement strict order (cancellation) and position limits, or prohibit certain market activities. Very much in line with state-capitalist logic, China's exchanges/regulators are relatively aggressive in their actions to curtail HFT, especially punishing foreign traders for rule violations (Reuters, 2017). While more prevalent in Indian markets, authorities have also been eager to regulate HFT, for instance, by introducing a transaction tax on trading or speed bumps (Meyer & Guernsey, 2015, 180–181). Especially since the emergence of

---

[39] See www.fia.org/data-resources.

a corruption scandal around HFT, regulatory scrutiny has further increased (Narayan, 2021). In contrast, Russia and Brazil have been very encouraging of HFT since the early 2010s. Russia's MOEX, for example, actively facilitates HFT through infrastructural arrangements such as unfiltered DMA, extensive colocation facilities or easier API access through the Financial Information eXchange (FIX) protocol (Madan, 2015). Brazil similarly strongly encourages HFT by upgrading market infrastructure to enable faster trading and removing its financial transaction tax (Mellow, 2014). As Andy Nybo, a Tabb Group analyst, noted, "they really have been aggressive in welcoming all types of [HFT] strategies" (Horch & Popper, 2013). Importantly, however, since 2022, HFT in Russia is now limited to domestic traders and those from "friendly countries," excluding all Western HFT powerhouses. In South Africa, HFT is also somewhat encouraged by the exchange, while the authorities do not regulate HFT individually either, preventing the possibility of constraining it. Overall, Chinese market infrastructures are most restrictive for HFT, and India also has a more cautious approach, whereas market infrastructures are designed to aggressively facilitate HFT in Russia and Brazil, while South Africa's stance is ambiguous.

At the international level, financial markets are regulated through two sets of international organizations. On the one hand, public international organizations such as the Financial Stability Board (FSB) or the International Organization of Securities Commissions (IOSCO) serve as discussion and regulatory fora for financial regulators. On the other hand, financial industry associations formed by financial market participants enable industry standard setting in stock markets (World Federation of Exchanges; WFE), derivative markets (Futures Industry Association; FIA) or central clearing (CCP12). Importantly, the growing size of financial markets in the BRICS (Figure 1) has bestowed them with a certain degree of influence in both types of institutions. Especially since the GFC, we can see a greater engagement of the BRICS with international financial market governance.

This was, for instance, reflected in the creation of the FSB in 2009. While its predecessor, the Financial Stability Forum, was initially a forum for only the G7 countries, in the course of the GFC, the scope and membership were widened to reflect a changing global financial system and included the G20 – most notably the BRICS. As Larionova and Shelepov (2022) note, "[the BRICS] regarded the G20–FSB cooperation as a key mechanism for shaping new global financial governance." Backing the reform agenda, they consequently made a substantive input into the decision-making process and lobbied for reducing possible negative effects of the new regulation on EMEs. Similarly, in 2009 China, Brazil and India were invited to join IOSCO's Technical Committee as changes within the international financial system needed to be reflected in "the composition of [IOSCO's] membership" (Reuters, 2009). Importantly, this gave the BRICS countries a greater voice in debates on public standard setting in financial markets (Henning & Walter, 2016). For financial industry associations, we can also observe increasing BRICS engagement. While in the 2000s the BRICS were virtually absent from these associations, since the GFC, both state-owned and private financial actors from the BRICS have increasingly become sponsors, exhibitors, speakers and even hosts of industry association events. In addition, BRICS exchanges have repeatedly held the WFE Chairmanship, and the newly founded organization of clearing houses, CCP12, is headquartered in Shanghai as China wanted to increase its power in international standard setting. Thereby, both private and also state-owned financial actors from the BRICS are able to partake in and influence industry discussions on best practices and standard setting. While virtually absent a few years ago, they now have a seat at the table and can gradually influence financial market regulation.

3.6 Accounting Standards

Various parts of the GFO – particularly in the financial sub-order – rely on the support of accounting practices. Accounting standards are crucial to provide investors, lenders and other company stakeholders with reliable information on the financial situation of a company. However, there is considerable disagreement globally about the most suitable accounting standards.

On the <u>domestic</u> level, accounting standards are closely linked to different types of capitalism (Nölke & Perry, 2007a; Perry & Nölke, 2006). Liberal capitalism as in the UK and the US goes hand-in-hand with the so-called model of fair value accounting (FVA). In FVA, accounting standards are crucial to provide outsider investors with the most transparent information about companies' well-being. The alternative is historic cost accounting (HCA), which is more conservative and prudent. The lower degree of transparency also allows for the hiding of slack resources from investors, as a cushion for hard times. Correspondingly, it is in line with types of capitalism that focus on long-term corporate development, including high investments in production and human resource development. These are typical features of not only coordinated market economies (CMEs) like Germany but also state capitalism in large emerging economies. In the latter, families or the state are major owners, not financial investors. The same applies to the favorable features of HCA with regard to long-term credit relations with banks – typical features not only of the German CME but also of state capitalism. On the one hand, HCA assists in making sure that there are sufficient revenues and collateral to protect bank loans. On the other hand, banks in long-term credit relationships as insiders have other sources of information about the economic well-being of companies and do not require the type of transparency provided by FVA, a hallmark of the liberal GFO. All BRICS deviate from FVA but to different degrees. Although China has formally adopted FVA – previously prohibited – in the process of formal convergence on global accounting standards, substantial convergence remains limited, particularly for nonfinancial long-term assets (Peng & Bewley, 2010). Similar observations have to be made for Russia: Again, a formal convergence on global FVA-based accounting standards often is evaded by practitioners who prefer to stick to the more traditional (HCA) approach (Combs et al., 2013). Also in India, practitioners prefer HCA over FVA, except for property investment (Chadda & Vardia, 2020). Even in Brazil (Silva et al., 2021) and South Africa (Pandya et al., 2021), where global standards have been formally adapted, practitioners prefer HCA given the choice, since the latter is more in line with their type of capitalism. By and large, the BRICS resist pressures to conform with liberal accounting standards.

In a transnational perspective, the core question is how comprehensively countries apply the accounting standards ("International Financial Reporting Standards/IFRS") by the International Accounting Standards Board (IASB), a private standard-setter located in London. The IASB is well known for the application of liberal FVA standards, even if powerful interests opposed the latter in the past (Nölke & Perry, 2007b). For two decades, we have been witnessing an attempt for the global harmonization of national accounting standards. In this process, the IASB has become the de facto global standard-setter. However, countries differ considerably with regard to their full application of IFRS. Some countries adopt the latter fully, others reserve national modifications and China has national standards that are only "substantially converged with IFRS." The IASB website provides jurisdictional profiles that detail the degree of IFRS adoption according to several criteria. Concerning the commitment to IFRS, the core question is on the adoption with or without exceptions ("carve-outs"). The IFRS may be required for domestic or foreign companies, or both. Countries may reserve the right for a formal endorsement of new standards by a national legislator or standard-setter, or simply automatically apply these standards. Particularly controversial are IFRS for small- and medium-scale enterprises (SMEs), in contrast to large exchange-listed companies where there is a broader agreement. The comparison of different degrees of IFRS support demonstrates that state-capitalist economies – in particular China and India – continue to resist the transnational spread of accounting standards that are wedded to liberal capitalism (Table 7, see also Ghio & Verona, 2015).

Table 7 Degree of IFRS support in different jurisdictions.

	UK	US[40]	S. Africa	Brazil	Russia	India	China
(1) IFRS adoption	2	2	2	2	2	1	0
(2) Extent of IFRS application	2	2	2	2	2	0	0
(3) IFRS endorsement	2[41]	2	2	1	1	0	0
(4) IFRS for SME	1	1	1	1	0	0	0
(5) Total	**7**	**7**	**7**	**6**	**5**	**1**	**0**

Explanation: (1) 2 = adoption without carve-outs, 1 = adoption with carve-outs, 0 = no adoption; (2) 2 = required for domestic and foreign companies, 1 = only domestic or only foreign; (3) 2 = no national endorsement necessary, 1 = national endorsement necessary; (4) 1 = adoption, 0 = no adoption; (5) sum of 1–4.

Source: *Authors' table; evaluations based on text statements in IFRS (2023).*

[40] For historical reasons, the US have their own set of accounting standards, the General Accepted Accounting Principles (GAAP). Technically speaking, they do not commit, endorse and apply IFRS. However, with regard to the core question of FVA, the approaches of IFRS and GAAP are identical. Correspondingly, GAAP commitment/ endorsement/application is considered equivalent to IFRS for the purpose of this study.
[41] Regulation before Brexit. Since Brexit, the UK requires a separate national endorsement.

In order to make cross-border capital mobility as simple as possible for investors, on the <u>international</u> level, the liberal GFO requires one central global standard. Moreover, an institution of private governance that is managed by private financial institutions should ideally set this standard to make sure that its standards are in line with the preferences of the transnational financial investor community. The IASB and its IFRS follows this idea very closely (Nölke & Perry, 2007b). The BRICS countries and other large emerging economies have articulated their concerns about the global centralization of accounting standard setting along liberal lines. They rather prefer a prominent role for national governments and an adaption of international accounting standards to their domestic economic models. Correspondingly, they have demanded a reform of the IASB, particularly after the GFC that had been intensified by FVA application in the US financial sector. In negotiation with Western governments, the BRICS governments succeeded with some reforms very quickly (Nölke, 2010). These reforms inter alia included the establishment of an intergovernmental "monitoring board" supervising the private governance of the IASB, the requirement of the IASB to report to the intergovernmental FSB and a broader geographical representation on the IASB, reducing the overwhelming majority held by Anglo-Saxon member countries.

Correspondingly, the BRICS – in particular China – not only succeeded in moderating the comprehensive application of liberal accounting standards on the domestic level but also made sure that they are in a more powerful position in global accounting standard setting in the future. However, their role of the day-to-day work of the IASB still remains limited (Nölke, 2015b). Moreover, we can see some differences with regard to the roles that BRICS members are playing in the governance of the IASB, largely representing a combination of their political power and proximity to core powers and principles of the IASB (Ramanna, 2013, 29–33). While the Board still is dominated by members stemming from Anglo-Saxon economies (US, UK, Australia and Canada), three of the BRICS are represented (Brazil, China, and South Africa), whereas two abstain (India and Russia).[42] Arguably, the former three can be classified as reformers and the remaining two as contestants. This is also in line with a "geopolitical" perspective on international accounting standard setting (Camfferman, 2020), which notes a significant absence of Russia and an active reformist role of China, in spite of considerable divergence from the IASB standards. More recently, China has even stepped up its potential contestation of the IASB, by convening a "Belt and Road countries accounting standards cooperation forum" (with the participation of Russia) in Xiamen in 2019. Given that this forum "positions itself as more distant from the IASB . . . it

---

[42] See www.iasplus.com/en/resources/ifrsf/iasb-ifrs-ic/iasb-board.

is clear that accounting standards are not out of scope in China's overall policy of creating international cooperative networks in which itself can play a leading role" (Camfferman, 2020, 254–255).

4 Contestation of the Development Sub-order

In any GFO, specific issue areas exist that pertain to lower income countries (developing and emerging economies). Importantly, these institutional configurations are crucial in structuring the relationship between developing and developed countries, potentially cementing global financial hierarchies and power constellations. On the short-term macroeconomic level, continuing balance-of-payment problems lead to indebtedness to international creditors. These creditor–debtor relationships are then managed by specific institutions and might be linked to specific conditionalities. Further, developing countries also require more long-term project financing to facilitate continued economic development. Here again, financing may stem from very different sources and may be provided under different conditions. As the following sections demonstrate, we can see considerable contestation from the BRICS on different levels of these two issue areas.

4.1 International Debt Management

The relationship between creditors and debtors as well as between assets and liabilities is central to the functioning of financial markets (Braun & Koddenbrock, 2021; Graeber, 2011). How debt is managed internationally is therefore an important pillar of GFOs. This debt management is handled by IFIs, national governments and private investors such as commercial banks. In the contemporary GFO, there is a strong role for the IMF (IFIs), Paris Club (national governments) and London Club (commercial banks) that are designed to strengthen claim enforcement against national governments on behalf of private investors. If governments cannot serve their debt, claim enforcement is thereby accompanied with deepening liberalization (SAPs) with the aim of making governments more efficient and adhering to market-based principles. This is not just the case for the Global South, but also for developed countries themselves as the Eurozone crisis demonstrated. In contrast, state-capitalist logic rather advocates for a weak role of global institutions and private financial actors. Instead, bilateral negotiations between national governments are preferred. Further, there is a preference for abstaining from liberalization efforts and instead advocating economic partnerships that facilitate national economic development.

We thereby see significant <u>domestic</u> divergence between the BRICS and liberal countries. This is especially important since the BRICS have emerged as major global creditors. Between 2010 and 2019, more than half of bilateral loans to developing countries came from the BRICS, especially from China (USD243.7 billion) and Russia (USD90.7 billion) and to a lesser extent from India (USD24.3 billion) and Brazil (<USD10 billion) (World Bank, 2021). But while the UK and, especially, the US have spearheaded structural adjustment and conditionality as crucial conditions in international debt management, the BRICS are decidedly against imposing conditionalities, especially in the form of SAPs (Ban & Blyth, 2013). This is because, except China, all BRICS countries have experienced the adverse effects of IMF conditionality themselves (India in 1991, Brazil in 2002, South Africa in 2020, and Russia in 1998). Further, besides Russia, the BRICS economies share a colonial past, which has a significantly impact on how they view global hierarchies and power relations that structure the financial relationships between core and periphery.[43] By defining themselves as developing countries, the BRICS emphasize South-South Cooperation, the principle of "noninterference" and fair relationships that defy what they consider a paternalistic or postcolonial practice (Barone & Spratt, 2015, 14).

This difference also translates into bilateral transnational debt relations between the BRICS and debtor countries. Rather than forcing the implementation of SAPs that aim to liberalize recipient countries' economies, the terms of short-term debt restructuring from BRICS countries include measures that further the donors' national development goals without interfering into the recipient countries' economic policy. A case in point here would be China's takeover of strategic infrastructures (that it helped finance) such as the Hambantota International Port in Sri Lanka. Faced with a short-term balance-of-payment crisis in 2017 since several of its international sovereign bonds were about to mature, Sri Lanka was in need for USD liquidity. It consequently leased a 70% stake of the port to the China Merchants Port Holdings Company for ninety-nine years for USD 1.12 billion. Rather than paying for the construction of an unsustainable infrastructure project (as often discussed in the "debt trap diplomacy" discourse), Sri Lanka used the much-needed USD-infusion by Chinese actors to service its debt to international investors (Moramudali, 2019; Moramudali, 2020).[44] Similarly to China, Russia uses debt relief for political purposes. In July 2023, for instance, Russia granted USD 684 million in debt relief to Somalia as Russia "seeks to . . .

---

[43] Brazil was colonized by Portugal, while India and South Africa were mostly under British rule. After the Opium wars, Chinese port cities were occupied by different Western powers and Hong Kong was under British rule.

[44] While China was Sri Lanka's single largest creditor, it held only around 10% of Sri Lanka's international debt, compared to private financial actors that held 47% of its debt; www.erd.gov .lk/index.php?option=com_content&view=article&id=102&Itemid=308&lang=en (last accessed February 2, 2023).

bolster relations with African nations and push back against Western efforts to isolate Moscow over its invasion of Ukraine."[45] Besides China and Russia, other BRICS economies have not been very active in debt management outside of the Paris Club and it is hence difficult to assess how their rhetoric might translate into actual policies.

The BRICS only partially support the international institutions responsible for international debt management like the Paris Club, created by the US and Europe in 1956. Only Russia and Brazil are Paris Club members, joining in 1997 and 2016, respectively, while India, China and South Africa only have status as ad hoc participants. Whereas Russia, Brazil and South Africa have each participated in a series of debt treatments, the Paris Club lists no engagement from India or Brazil.[46] However, not only do the BRICS not fully support the Paris Club, but China also actively undermines it. As Gelpern et al. (2021, 6–7) note in their analysis of Chinese debt contracts, "close to three-quarters of the debt contracts … contain what we term 'No Paris Club' clauses, which expressly commit the borrower to exclude the debt from restructuring in the Paris Club of official bilateral creditors, and from any comparable debt treatment." Further, the severing of diplomatic ties between China and the debtor constitutes an event of default in Chinese debt contracts. Rather than solely determined by market events, Chinese debt contracts are thereby also politicized, highlighting qualitative differences in debt management regimes. While data on debt held by other BRICS countries is scarce, it is noteworthy that debt contracts with Indian creditors share similar provisions that define the termination of diplomatic relations as an event of default (Gelpern et al., 2022, 43), indicating that the politicization of debt could extend beyond Chinese lending.

This is especially relevant given the transformation of the international debt management regime (Figure 12). While developed countries (Paris Club) and multilateral institutions (especially the IMF) historically held a large portion of developing countries' debt, this has changed in recent years. Between 2000 and 2021, the share of the Paris Club fell from 55% to 18%. At the same time, private bondholders also became the largest holders of developing country debt rising from 10% to 50%, while China emerged as a major creditor, increasing its share from 1% to 15% and outpacing IMF, Paris Club and World Bank.

China's approach has thereby provided a mixed picture. On the one hand, China has repeatedly forgiven noninterest-bearing loans to developing countries, which should be classified as official development assistance and account

---

[45] www.reuters.com/world/africa/somalia-says-russia-grants-relief-debt-worth-684-million-2023-07-27/ (last accessed November 9, 2023).

[46] See https://clubdeparis.org/en/communications/page/ad-hoc-participants (last accessed March 21, 2022).

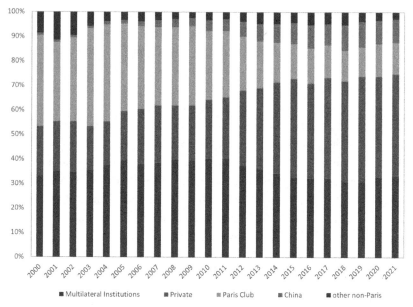

Figure 12 External debt of poorer countries by creditor (2000–2021).
Source: *World Bank data.*

for 5% of China's loan commitments (Mitchell, 2022), most recently twenty-three loans to seventeen African countries worth USD 1.5 billion in 2022. As China's *Global Times* newspaper argues (Islam, 2022), "there are fundamental differences between Chinese debt relief, and debt relief from the US and its controlled global financial institutions [since] China does not involve itself in the internal political mechanism of any country [and that] instead of colonialism, China provides 'solidarity' between developing countries." On the other hand, China has forgiven only very little interest-bearing debt, which is usually held by Chinese banks. The approach has rather been to restructure debt and prolong the repayment period, albeit without demanding domestic political reforms. One interpretation of this behavior could be that rather than pushing for liberalization, China's debt management is more (geo)politically motivated as it seeks greater political influence with its debtor countries. This would go along with recent studies that demonstrate how increased Chinese financial flows correlate with countries' voting alignment in the UN (Raess et al., 2017; Stone et al., 2022).

It is important to note that private bondholders (mostly Western institutional investors), which hold the majority of developing country debt, have not engaged in debt restructuring or relief since they want to be paid in full and not write down their investments (Figure 13). While China has thus been

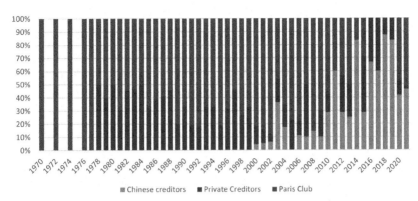

Figure 13 Participation in international debt restructuring (1970–2021).
Source: *Data from Horn et al. (2022); authors' calculation.*

criticized for not granting enough debt relief and relying on restructuring ("kicking the can down the road"; The Economist, 2022), there is a marked difference between dominant liberal debt management regime and China's approach.

4.2 Development Finance

The final building block of GFOs is development finance –how states utilize finance on preferential terms to facilitate economic development both at home and abroad. This pertains to the role of NatDBs, both domestically and concerning their transnational activities, bilateral development assistance between countries as well as the construction of multilateral development banks as international institutions that – next to providing a substantial share of development financing – also shape the norms according to which such financing takes place. From a liberal perspective, development finance plays a minor role domestically, largely coordinated through official development assistant (ODA) between countries on the transnational level, while international authority is concentrated in the World Bank with which regional development banks (and bilateral donors) coordinate. Development financing is thereby either charitable (ODA) or focuses on the commercial viability of projects, the latter being funded by market-based interest rates. Both forms usually come with strings attached. Especially since the 1980s, with the emergence of the (post-) Washington Consensus as the globally dominant development paradigm, Western development assistance has been conditional and tied to (neo)liberal SAPs of fiscal policy discipline, tax reform, market-base interest and exchange rates, trade and investment liberalization, deregulation, securing property rights and financial deregulation (Williamson, 1993). In contrast, development finance is much more important domestically within state-capitalist economies, provided by very powerful public development banks. Rather than "charitable" ODA, bilateral development finance utilizes different mechanisms and focuses on both commercial viability and political objectives, while new international institutions are created that operate independently and create different norms from the World Bank.

Analyzing the size and growth of NatDBs, we can observe significant domestic variation between countries. Representing an increasing share of global banking, NatDBs account for 6.5% of global banking assets in 2018. This growth of NatDBs, however, can largely be attributed to the rise of the BRICS (and other Asian countries; see Pape & Petry, 2024) where they have emerged as an important policy tool. Although one can observe a growing importance of development banks *within* Continental Europe (Mertens et al., 2021), in comparison, NatDBs are far less important in Western economies than in the BRICS. According to data on the fifty largest development banks from the *Sovereign Wealth Fund Institute* (SWFI),[47] the US and UK only accounted for 0.01% and 0.15% of development bank assets;[48] in contrast, the BRICS accounted for 68.28% (SWFI, 2023). While South Africa's development bank lending is on par with the UK (0.1–0.15%), the share of India (0.77%), Russia (0.92%) and Brazil (2.42%) is significantly higher, while China outpaces everyone else (64.08%), having emerged as the single largest source of development finance globally. Not only in absolute terms but also in relative terms with respect to their national economies, we can see large differences. NatDB assets account for only 0.04% and 2.56% of US and UK GDP, respectively. This is much higher in the BRICS, albeit with some variation. In India (16.15%) and South Africa (16.69%), NatDBs play a comparably smaller role; they are much more important in Russia (34.55%) and Brazil (93.6%) and have an outsized role in China (243.15%). Overall, NatDBs play a much more important role in the BRICS than in liberal countries.

Importantly, we can also observe increasing transnational activities of development finance from the BRICS with seemingly different characteristics. In the liberal GFO, development assistance is often tied to SAPs aimed at good governance and market-friendly institutional reforms under the *OECD's Development Assistance Committee* (DAC) framework. As Dreher et al. (2013, 403) note, for a long time, the DAC has been "*the* major institution that sets the aid agenda." Yet, since the 2000s, we can observe the rise of

---

[47] This data comprises the fifty largest development banks by total assets; next to NatDBs, this figure includes regional development banks such as the ADB or EBRD but excludes the World Bank.

[48] Continental Europe accounts for 13.78%; thereof Germany's KfW for 12.01% alone.

development finance from non-DAC countries, which Woods (2008, 16) describes as "a silent revolution [that] is taking place in the development assistance regime." BRICS development agencies usually do not impose any strict policy conditionalities; they operate outside of the DAC regulations and development finance is rather directed at facilitating national development objectives.

Brazilian development assistance – provided by the Brazilian Cooperation Agency and other public bodies – is geared toward the promotion of domestic preferences, particularly commercial interests (e.g. agriculture), domestic political priorities (social policy issues like education, health, etc.) and foreign policy (leadership in Latin America), and the DAC agenda and the interferences into the national sovereignty of recipient countries are explicitly opposed (Asmus et al., 2017, 7–10). Investment projects by Russia's VEB bank are often located in Central Asia and Eastern Europe, and favorable financing conditions are given for investments in strategically important sectors such as commodities, mining or resource extraction (Holtbrügge & Kreppel, 2012). South Africa provides some assistance to countries in Sub-Saharan Africa, focusing on regional economic interests but with smaller volumes and a focus on conflict-prone countries (Asmus et al., 2017, 23–26). For India, geopolitical influence in Africa and especially (South) Asia is an important driver of development finance, especially regional competition with China; a recent analysis of ExIm Bank lending patterns, for instance, highlighted how Indian development finance often follows prominent Chinese investments in specific regions (Asmus et al., 2021), with Sri Lanka being a recent example. Finally, Chinese development finance is driven by a multitude of political factors such as gaining political influence in Asia, furthering economic interests in Africa – including access to commodities – or financing the Belt and Road Initiative (AidData, 2021). As Lauria and Fumagalli (2019) note, the BRICS "share the ideals of political non-interference and win-win cooperation" but "their approaches to development assistance differ in their volumes, drivers, tools, and modality." Still, there are marked contrasts to the liberal GFO's development assistance, particularly rejecting the DAC approach and policy conditionality.[49] Moreover, BRICS development financing follows more strategic-political motives that favor domestic national development objectives (Barone & Spratt, 2015; Asmus et al., 2017, 4–7).

When it comes to the <u>international</u> level, development finance has long been regulated and coordinated by US-dominated IFIs in the Global North like DAC or

---

[49] While Chinese loans might have a degree of "project-based" conditionalities, these are not directed at liberalizing host country institutions but rather at securing Chinese national development interest through project-based financing.

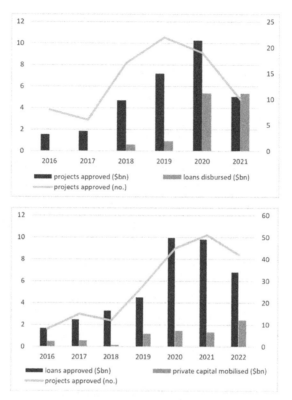

Figure 14 Development of AIIB (a) and NewDB (b), 2016–2022.
Source: *AIIB/NewDB annual reports; no 2022 data available for NewDB.*

the World Bank. Since the GFC, the BRICS, however, have also engaged in creating new international institutions for development finance, most prominently the BRICS NewDB in 2014 and the China-led Asian Infrastructure Investment Bank (AIIB) in 2016. Both institutions experienced significant growth, rapidly increasing the number of financed projects, loan dispersion and capital mobilization (Figure 14), already accounting for 4% of multilateral lending by 2018 (OECD, 2020) although their growth has slowed down since. Importantly, both the NewDB and the AIIB have vowed to not impose conditionalities on their loans (Creutz, 2023; Qing, 2015), reflecting the principle of "noninterference" that the BRICS already follow with respect to international debt management.

The BRICS reject conditionality as paternalist interference in the domestic affairs of recipient countries, representing a significant departure from liberal norms, fundamentally challenging international institutions in the area of development finance. Importantly, this also affects the activities of liberal institutions themselves. Hernandez (2017), for instance, finds that the World

Bank attaches fewer conditions to its loans when a recipient country receives significant amounts of Chinese development finance (also Zeitz, 2021). Finally, the BRICS also challenge the governance model of the institutions of the liberal GFO: Similar to the case of the CRA (see Section 2.2), the NDB is based on an equal sharing of voting rights between the five member countries (Wang, 2017, 116); the AIIB, in contrast, clearly is dominated by China (Wang, 2019). Overall, the BRICS – especially China – are thus increasingly reshuffling the liberal principles of global development.

5 Conclusion: The External Contestation of Liberalism

What have we learned about the contemporary GFO and its contestation through the BRICS? After developing a conceptual framework to systematically analyze the GFO, its constituting elements, contemporary liberal form and state-capitalist theoretical alternative, the empirical sections of this Element delved into empirical material to analyze the variegated nature of this contestation. Since this Element covers a lot of ground, the following sections summarize these findings, discuss their significance for contemporary debates on the BRICS and the fate of economic liberalism and also outline future avenues of research to further study this important development.

5.1 Summary of Empirical Results

The BRICS' contestation of the contemporary liberal GFO is not uniform across issue areas, levels of contestation or specific countries. Through our empirical analyses, we aimed to (1) identify which of the BRICS countries contests the liberal GFO, (2) in which issue areas the liberal GFO is contested and (3) whether this contestation takes place domestically, transnationally or in the realm of international institutions. The following section summarizes and discusses this variegated contestation by using heat maps, which allow us to visualize patterns of contestation. Overall, the contestation of liberalism is strongest and most widespread at the domestic and transnational levels and not quite as extensive on the international level.

On the domestic dimension (Table 8), we can observe stark variation with respect to state-capitalist contestation of the liberal GFO. For exchange rate regimes (Section 2.1), we can see significant variation with China, Russia and India, deviating the most from the liberal ideal of free-float.[50] When it comes to

---

[50] In the absence of numerical values, we categorized the type of system according to whether they correspond with the liberal (1) or state-capitalist (4) ideal type; with free-float closest to the liberal ideal type (1), followed by floating regimes with some intervention (2), managed float regimes (3) and managed regimes (4).

Table 8 State-capitalist contestation (domestic dimension).

	China	India	Russia	Brazil	S. Africa	US	UK
exchange rate regimes: rating 1-4	4	3	3	2	2	1	1
Balance of payments: FX reserves (% global)	26.1%	4.7%	4.2%	2.7%	0.5%	0.3%	0.9%
Balance of payments: FX reserves: rating 1-6	6	4	4	4	2	2	1
Balance of payments: FX reserves (% GDP)	17.5%	16.6%	22.2%	16.9%	15.0%	0.1%	3.6%
Monetary policy: rating 1-3	3	2	2	1	1	1	1
International capital mobility: Shinn-Ito Index	-1.23	-1.23	-0.16	-1.00	-1.23	2.31	2.31
Foreign direct investment: restrictiveness index	0.22	0.21	0.26	0.08	0.06	0.09	0.04
Corporate ownership: institutional investor ownership	20.6%	38.8%	22.5%	46.3%	54.3%	82.6%	78.1%
Corporate ownership: state ownership	42.5%	17.4%	34.9%	17.0%	9.1%	0.6%	4.6%
Banks: state-ownership (assets)	51.0%	70.0%	72.0%	41.0%	4.0%	0.0%	8.0%
Financial markets: state-ownership exchange	100.0%	30.0%	30.2%	0.0%	20.5%	0.0%	0.0%
Financial markets: competition	2	2	1	1	1	3	3
Accounting standards	3	3	3	2	2	1	1
International debt management: rating 1-3	3	3	2	2	3	1	1
Development finance: rating 1-6 (% global NatDB assets)	5	3	3	4	2	1	2
Development finance: rating 1-3 (NatDB assets % GDP)	5	2	3	4	2	1	1
Development finance: NatDB assets % GDP	243.2%	16.1%	34.5%	93.6%	16.7%	0.0%	0.0%

Source: *Authors' table; based on empirical subsections.*

FX reserves (Section 2.2), we see a mixed picture. China clearly accounts for the majority of FX reserves, but Brazil, Russia and India also have substantive holdings, which is clearly at odds with the liberal ideal.[51] Especially when comparing the relative size of FX reserve holdings compared to the respective countries' GDP, we can see that all BRICS countries, even South Africa, substantially diverge from the Anglo-American core. Big differences also exist with respect to central banking (Section 2.3). Here, central banks range from (1) being completely independent as propagated by the liberal paradigm, (2) having compromised independence to (3) being explicitly subordinated to state policy.[52] Overall, China is emerging as the clearest contestant of the monetary sub-order, while India and Russia follow more state-capitalist than liberal principles, with Brazil as a mixed case and South Africa quite close to the liberal ideal type represented by the US and UK.

In contrast, we can observe much more consistent contestation through the BRICS in the domestic level of the finance sub-order. With regard to international capital mobility (Section 3.1), all BRICS countries have closed capital accounts despite periods of liberalization, while Western markets liberalized to a degree where almost no barriers to the entry of financial capital exist. This picture is not as clear when it comes to FDI (Section 3.2). Despite significant opening, China, India and Russia contest the liberal principle of unrestricted FDI flows and remain some of the most restricted destinations for FDI investments globally, whereas South Africa and Brazil have similarly liberal regimes like the US and UK. On the issue of corporate ownership (Section 3.3), we can again observe a similar picture where state ownership is high in Russia, India and China, moderate in Brazil and South Africa and almost nonexistent in the US and UK, with a reverse picture when it comes to ownership by institutional investors, the epitomization of liberal capital markets. In connection to banking (Section 3.4), state ownership is very high in the BRICs, while South Africa is in the liberal camp with very low state ownership.

For the organization of financial markets (Section 3.5), we can observe two patterns. State ownership of exchanges is absolute in China, substantial in India, Russia and South Africa and nonexistent in Brazil, the US and UK. However, we see no or only managed competition between trading platforms in the

---

[51] When using absolute values, China's outsized FX reserves obfuscate the significance of other holdings; categorizing holdings on an ordinal scale based on their share of total FX reserves provides a more nuanced picture; very small (1; >0.1%), small (2; 0.1–1%), medium (3; 1–2.5%), substantive (4; 2.5–5%) and very substantive (5; 5–10%) to huge (6; >10%).

[52] We coded these characteristics as ordinal values: central bank independence (1), compromised independence (2) to dependence (3).

BRICS, in contrast to fragmented markets in the US and UK.[53] Finally, with respect to accounting standards (Section 3.6), we see considerable divergence from liberal standards in China, India and Russia, which often follow HCA, and partial divergence in Brazil and South Africa, while the US and UK have fully adopted FVA.[54] Overall, with respect to the finance sub-order, we can see higher degrees of contestation from all BRICS countries, albeit not in each issue area. Especially Russia and India have thereby emerged as important contestants of the liberal order next to China, with Brazil as a mixed case and South Africa more often following liberal principles.

Finally, with respect to the development sub-order, we have a twofold picture. On the one hand, we can observe that the BRICS in general follow more state-capitalist than liberal rules when it comes to the principles of development finance. This can be seen both in their rejection of SAPs when it comes to international debt management (Section 4.1)[55] as well as the prominent role of NatDBs (Section 4.2).[56] On the other hand, it is important to notice that while the BRICS might individually contest the liberal development paradigm on a programmatic level, China stands out as the most serious challenger due to its vast footprint in development finance.

A similar pattern of contestation emerges with respect to the transnational dimension (Table 9). For exchange rate regimes (Section 2.1), Brazil, Russia and India follow more state-capitalist principles with limited offshore trading of their currencies, with China as a mixed case and South Africa in the liberal camp.[57] A different picture emerges with respect to balance of payments (Section 2.2) where China and India create alternative swap line networks beyond the Fed-based liberal system, Russia and South Africa being integrated into the Chinese and not the liberal network and Brazil only integrated into the Fed network.[58] Similarly, when analyzing CBDCs – which we see as a more

---

[53] We coded the different competition patterns according to the following scheme: no competition (1), managed competition (2) and extensive competition (3) on the state-capitalist (1) to liberal (3) spectrum.

[54] We coded the different accounting standard regimes as comprehensive implementation of FVA (1), comprehensive adaption of FVA, but preference for HCA if discretion for preparers (2); and comprehensive formal adaption of FVA, but informal practice often HCA (3).

[55] We coded countries based on whether they approve of SAPs and are Paris Club members (1), whether they are Paris Club members but officially do not approve of SAPs (2) or whether they are not Paris Club members and officially refuse SAPs (3).

[56] Since China has an outsized quantitative footprint in the development sub-order, we also coded countries on an ordinal scale to assess qualitative differences between their approaches.

[57] For this issue area, we coded the MSCI ratings from least open (state-capitalist) to most open (liberal), i.e. "–/?" (3), "+" (2) and "++" (1).

[58] We coded these as creation of alternative swap line network/not part of Fed network (3), integration into alternative swap line network/not part of Fed network (2) and not part of alternative network/integrated into Fed network (1).

Table 9 State-capitalist contestation (transnational dimension).

	China	India	Russia	Brazil	S. Africa	US	UK
exchange rate regimes: rating 1-3	2	3	3	3	1	1	1
Balance of payments: rating 1-3	3	3	2	1	2	1	1
Monetary policy: CBDC rating 1-3	3	3	3	2	1	1	1
International capital mobility: rating 1-3	3	3	3	2	1	1	1
Foreign direct investment: rating 1-3	3	1	2	1	1	1	1
Corporate ownership: ownership pattern	5%	20%	25%	43%	52%	21.3%	74.82%
Corporate ownership: state-cap ownership rating	5	4	5	5	3	1	2
Banks: foreign-bank ownership (% assets)	1.0%	5.9%	6.3%	10.7%	6.0%	11.1%	36.6%
Banks: advanced-developing country lending ratio	0.10	0.31	0.78	0.17	0.33	1.56	1.34
Financial markets: spread of HFT score 1-3	3	2	3	1	2	1	7
Accounting standards	0	1	5	6	7	7	7
International debt management: rating 1-2	2	3	2	3	1	1	1
Development finance: rating 1-3	3	3	3	3	3	1	1

Source: *Authors' table; based on empirical subsections.*

state-capitalist monetary policy tool – in Section 2.3, India, Russia and China have the most advanced projects, followed by Brazil while South Africa, the US and UK have made comparatively little progress on this matter. Overall, we can clearly see China and India leading the transnational contestation of the liberal GFO in the monetary sub-order.

Similar to the domestic dimension, we can observe the most significant overall challenge of the liberal GFO in the finance sub-order on the trans-national level. With respect to capital mobility (Section 3.1), China, India and Brazil stand out as cases that are threatened to be downgraded based on their restrictions on offshore financial products, whereby China and India have contested these liberal norms more directly and all Russian indices have been discontinued after it changed its investment policies.[59] With respect to FDI (Section 3.2), we can observe high degrees of more strategically oriented outward investment in China and (to a lesser degree) Russia, while FDI from other countries is less pronounced and more market-driven. For corporate ownership (Section 3.3), we can again observe more contestation. On the one hand, foreign ownership of BRICS companies is (very) low in China, India and Russia and relatively high in Brazil and South Africa. On the other hand, the BRICs emerge as important owners with respect to state-led transnational investment, which pursues strategically oriented investments.[60] With respect to banking (Section 3.4), on the one hand, we can see state-capitalist ideals embodied in the (very) low market shares of foreign banks in China, India, Russia and South, while Brazil has a similar market share to the US (but not as high as the UK). When it comes to the lending activity of BRICS banks, on the other hand, we can see a clear divide where especially China and Brazil, but also India and South Africa and to a lesser degree Russia, have very different lending patterns to Anglo-American banks as they predominantly lend to developing markets outside the liberal core. The picture becomes less clear for the financial markets (Section 3.5) where we investigate HFT. Here, Brazil has been fully embracing this liberal ideal, while India and South Africa and especially China and Russia have hampered the transnational spread of this market practice.[61] Finally, we can see that India and China have not followed the IFRS' trans-national accounting standard practices (Section 3.7), while the other BRICS do more or less comply with these liberal ideas. Overall, transnational contestation

---

[59] We coded cases for whether they comply with index providers' liberal rules (1), violate them and are hence on a watch list (2) or actively contest the authority of index providers (3).

[60] State-led investment is coded from liberal (1) to more strategical/state-capitalist (5) as: liberal portfolio (1), portfolio/majority (2), minority (3), minority/majority (4) and strategic majority (5) investment.

[61] We coded countries according to their permissiveness of HFT as supportive (1), some restrictions (2) and more substantial restrictions (3).

of the finance sub-order is quite substantial with China emerging as the most important and consistent challenger, while especially India and Russia and, to a lesser degree, Brazil complement China's contestation to varying degrees in each issue area.

Finally, when it comes to the development sub-order, we can see China and Russia taking on a different policy stance than the US and UK with respect to international debt management (Section 4.1).[62] Concerning development finance, we then see a significant divergence between the BRICS and Western countries. On the one hand, the BRICS uniformly reject liberal conditionalities and advocate noninterference in host countries. On the other hand, their sizable development banks (see domestic dimension) all conduct more strategic investments that further state objectives.[63]

China clearly challenges the liberal GFO across all dimensions, while India and Russia again share a lot of state-capitalist characteristics and export them transnationally. Brazil and South Africa are again mixed cases that combine both liberal and state-capitalist elements, with South Africa leaning slightly more toward the liberal side that is clearly represented by the US and UK. However, contestation is pronounced across the BRICS in a few areas: The BRICS are all active in creating CBDCs, transnational state-capitalist ownership clearly diverges from liberal portfolio investment, foreign banks that increasingly penetrated global banking systems are held at bay, cross-border lending by the BRICS is clearly directed toward developing countries and development finance clearly breaks with the conditionality-driven Washington Consensus.

With respect to the international dimension (Table 10), the contestation pattern is more patchy and more difficult to measure in the absence of quantifiable data. We therefore coded contestation on whether cases (1) comply with the existing institutions of the LIO, (2) partially contest them for instance by attempting to reform them or (3) outrightly challenge them by creating alternative institutions that are more in line with state-capitalist ideas. Overall, contestation is smallest in this dimension as the emphasis was mostly on reforming existing institutions rather than creating state-capitalist alternatives.

For exchange rate regimes (Section 2.1), China is clearly proposing an alternative to the USD with the internationalization of the RMB. However, rather than outrightly challenging USD hegemony, the motivation is rather to

---

[62] Coded as supporting conditionalities (1) vs. strategic actions that facilitate state objectives (2); until the end of our observation period (2020), it is difficult to code the policy stance of other BRICS countries, since China was the only country involved in transnational debt management.

[63] We correspondingly coded these countries as supporting liberal conditionalities (1), rejecting conditionalities (2) and rejecting conditionalities while facilitating strategic investment (3).

Table 10 State-capitalist contestation (international dimension).

	China	India	Russia	Brazil	S. Africa	US	UK
exchange rate regimes	3	2	3	2	1	1	1
Balance of payments	3	3	3	3	3	1	1
Monetary policy	2	2	2	2	2	1	1
International capital mobility	2	2	2	2	2	1	1
Foreign direct investment	2	3	2	3	3	1	1
Corporate ownership	2	2	2			1	1
Banks	2	2	2	2	2	1	1
Financial markets	2	2	2	2	2	1	1
Accounting standards	2	3	3	2	2	1	1
International debt management	3	3	1	1	2	1	1
Development finance	3	3	3	3	3	1	1

Source: Authors' table; based on empirical subsections.

achieve a certain degree of autonomy. This is also the main motivation for increased de-dollarization in Russia and to a lesser extent in India and Brazil, whereby movements toward de-dollarization are quite small in South Africa despite joint BRICS rhetoric about the need of a multipolar currency system.[64] In contrast, we see a more joint BRICS effort to provide an alternative to the liberal balance-of-payment system (Section 2.2) with the creation of the CRA and the support of regional currency swap institutions (China and Russia).[65] Furthermore, the BRICS did not propose the creation of alternative institutions when it comes to central bank coordination (Section 2.3) but rather collectively aimed to reform existing practices.[66]

While we do see a joint BRICS effort with respect to international capital mobility (Section 3.1), especially China, India and Brazil being vocal critics that contested and influenced the IMF's policy stance on this issue, we do not see the creation of a state-capitalist alternative institution.[67] A different picture emerges with respect to the international FDI regime (Section 3.2). Here, China and Russia are largely supportive of ISDS and BITs although they try to use the system to facilitate state interests, while Brazil, South Africa and India have contested the liberal system and created alternative mechanisms.[68] In the regulation of SWFs (Section 3.3), in contrast, China, India and Russia have been quite successful in watering down international regulation, very much to the dismay of the US and UK, while Brazil and South Africa were not part of the process. Importantly, however, while the BRICS partially watered down liberal regulations, this was rather a defensive move and they did not proactively aim to shape SWF regulation in a state-capitalist logic.[69] For the area of international banking regulation (Section 3.4), we can observe joint efforts by the BRICS to lobby against very liberal private self-regulation of banks (as contained in Basel II) as well as activities for the creation of both domestic rating agencies and the potential creation of a BRICS rating agency that contest the liberal banking regime. However, neither were the BRICS able to establish more state-capitalist rules nor was the BRICS rating agency a big success. With respect to financial

---

[64] We thus coded countries as either trying to create alternative currency systems (3), partially de-dollarizing (2) or not contesting the USD (1).

[65] This joint initiative is coded as state-capitalist alternative (3) to existing liberal institutions (1).

[66] Since the BRICS are simply reforming existing liberal institutions (1), they are coded as partial contestation (2) rather than full contestation (3).

[67] In lieu of creating new institutions, we coded these actions as partial contestation through reform (2).

[68] We therefore coded China and Russia as reformers (2) and Brazil, South Africa and India as contestants (3).

[69] We coded cases according to whether they actively aimed to implement state-capitalist SWF regulation (3), watered-down liberal regulatory proposals (2) or whether pushed for liberal regulation (1); those countries without a stake in the process are left out of the analysis.

markets (Section 3.5), the BRICS have also become more important through their inclusion in the FSB as well as growing importance in IOSCO and industry standard-setting bodies, but rather attempting to have a voice criticism than creating alternative institutions. For accounting standards, Brazil, South Africa and especially China pushed for reforming liberal international institutions dominated by the US and UK while India and Russia have actively opted out of these liberal institutions.

While Brazil and Russia adhere to the liberal Paris Club, in international debt management (Section 4.1), China and India again emerge as the most severe contestants of the liberal GFO as they are not only not official members of the Paris Club (same as South Africa), but their debt contracts are also more politicized.[70] Finally, in development finance (Section 4.2), the creation of alternative institutions such as the BRICS-led NDB and the Chinese-led AIIB demonstrate a clear contestation of the Western development institutions and their emphasis on liberal conditionality.

Overall, the US and UK clearly represent the liberal spectrum, with the UK being closest to the liberal ideal type. The US only diverges significantly from the liberal ideal type with respect to foreign ownership of companies and banking assets – which makes sense since the global institutional investors (a hallmark of the liberal GFO) that dominate banking sectors and capital markets around the world are mostly US-based. South Africa and Brazil are mixed cases that combine many liberal elements but also some state-capitalist features such as high FX reserve accumulation (both), restrictions on international capital mobility (both), extensive development finance (Brazil) or state ownership of banks (Brazil); South Africa is thereby significantly more liberal across most measures. Russia, India and especially China are much more state-capitalist. Russia scores highest for state-capitalist characteristics such as state-owned banking assets, state ownership of companies and FDI restrictions on FX reserves, albeit also encompassing certain liberal trains such as high degrees of foreign ownership (before the Ukraine war), international capital mobility and floating exchange rates. India scores even more consistently higher on the state-capitalist scale, while China is closest to the state-capitalist ideal type. On the domestic dimension, Russia, India and China clearly emerge as the main challengers of the liberal GFO across almost all subcategories.

With respect to the questions that this Element addresses – in which issue areas, by whom and through which mechanisms the contemporary GFO is contested – the results are as follows. First, the GFO is contested across issue

---

[70] We coded cases on whether they are members of the liberal Paris Club (1), no official members (2) or which additionally also have politicized debt contracts (3).

areas albeit to varying degrees. Second, the Asian BRICS members – China, India and Russia – have emerged as the main contestants while Brazil and especially South Africa are more accommodating toward the liberal GFO. Third, most contestation occurs through the domestic and transnational levels, not so much the international level – on which most existing literature has focused. While the BRICS might find it challenging to jointly organize alternative multilateral institutions, we can definitely observe an increasing transnational spread of their state-capitalist financial practices.

5.2 Theoretical, Empirical and Political Significance of Findings

The GFO – "the rules, norms and procedures that govern cross-border money and finance" (Drezner & McNamara, 2013) – is a crucial component of contemporary economic liberalism. While currently hardly contested internally, we argue that the liberal GFO is increasingly subject to comprehensive external contestation through the financial rise of emerging markets. When this topic is analyzed, existing studies tend to overestimate or underestimate the extent of this challenge by focusing on individual countries (especially China) and/or individual issue areas such as multilateral development banks, currency internationalization or capital markets (Section 1). Addressing this inconsistency, this Element engages in a systematic analysis of this external contestation of the liberal GFO through emerging markets.

Theoretically, we therefore, first, defined the eleven constitutive elements of GFOs and the different dimensions where they can be contested, namely on the domestic, transnational and international levels. Second, we pinpointed the power constellations, ideas and institutions that underpin the contemporary *liberal* GFO. Third, we outlined the *state-capitalist* challenge to the liberal order that potentially stems from the rise of emerging markets. Table 11 summarizes the main differences between the liberal and the state-capitalist GFO in an ideal-typical way. The core focus of contemporary state capitalism is on supporting a process of catch-up industrialization under conditions of liberalized financial markets globally, a condition that usually goes under the heading of "financialization." On the macroeconomic and international levels, the core idea is the protection of national sovereignty against cross-border financial flows as a particularly aggressive form of liberal intrusiveness. Whereas on the microeconomic level, the core idea is the establishment of state restrictions that impede profit maximization for private agents and instead facilitate the accomplishment of certain state objectives. Domestic financial institutions make sure that finance serves as the target of catchup and implement limits on the ability of private actors to maximize profits.

Table 11 Different manifestations of global financial orders.

	Contemporary liberal GFO	State-capitalist alternative
Ideas (macro-level)	Free markets (e.g. free cross-border capital flows)	Protection of national sovereignty against cross-border financial flows
Ideas (micro-level)	Profit creation (e.g. maximize shareholder value)	Restrictions on profit maximization, instead of facilitation of state objectives
Power constellations	Wall Street/City of London, USD hegemony, Anglo-American investors	Preference for national autonomy, several power structures internationally
Institutions (macro-level)	Centralized financial institutions globally around Anglo-American core	Alternative financial infrastructures, reform of existing institutions
Institutions (micro-level)	Hands-off institutions domestically	Financial institutions make sure that finance serves national development objectives

Source: *Authors' table.*

Empirically, we thereby focus on the BRICS as the most important emerging markets that could embody such a contestation. We then systematically analyze varieties of contestation of the liberal GFO by investigating the eleven issue areas of the GFO across our three levels of contestation (domestic, transnational and international) for the BRICS economies as well as the US and UK (as benchmarks for liberal finance). Based on this analysis, we argue that we can observe considerable contestation across all three dimensions, with some variance.

First, China clearly emerges as the most important contestant, both in terms of qualitative (closest to the state-capitalist ideal type) and quantitative differences, in terms of its global impact. In contrast, Brazil and especially South Africa are mixed cases at best that combine both liberal and state-capitalist characteristics and do not make a significant global impact except in a few select individual issue areas. India and Russia, however, are decidedly more state-capitalist, contesting the liberal GFO both across many different issue areas as well as in terms of their global impact. Second, we can see significant variation with respect to issue areas. While we see considerable contestation in areas such as development finance, banking, corporate ownership and balance of payment, other issue areas such as financial markets or monetary policy are less systematically contested. Third, we can observe quite significant contestation when it comes to domestic ideas, power structures and institutional configurations but also with respect to the transnational spread of state-capitalist principles while resisting pressures to conform with liberal intrusiveness. In contrast, the international level is less clearly contested as the BRICS so far rather focus on reforming existing institutional arrangements than creating alternative state-capitalist ones. Fourth, we can observe an increasing contestation over time. In part, this is because in many issue areas domestic liberalization policies were reversed after the Asian or Global Financial Crises, and in part because the growing economic clout of the BRICS provided them with greater abilities to spread state-capitalist institutions transnationally. This is also because we can observe a growing awareness for collective identity and/or interests in some issue areas that have led to the creation of new international institutions.

Overall, we posit that the degree to which the liberal GFO is contested is much larger than is commonly acknowledged in the literature and only discernible if we consider the "big picture." Our systematic empirical analysis aims to fill this gap. We therefore hope that our systematic approach that combines both CPE and IPE in one coherent analytical framework (Nölke, 2023) to investigate variegated contestation across different dimensions of the GFO can also contribute to wider discussions on economic liberalism and its contestations. Our study thereby also sets a counterpoint to the discussion on financial subordination that currently is dominating the study of finance in emerging economies (Alami et al., 2023; Bonizzi et al., 2022). In contrast to the latter debate, our study demonstrates that some emerging markets can avoid a comprehensive subordination under the contemporary financial order. Instead, they might be able to resist liberal intrusiveness and its pressures to conform with Western standards and Anglo-American power constellations, creating a degree of autonomy or even the ability to facilitate their own state-capitalist ideas transnationally or internationally, as highlighted in discussions about financial statecraft (Armijo & Katada, 2014).

Politically, our study contains important implications for current discussions on the de-dollarization of the global economy. The global primacy of the dollar and its crucial importance for American power is a perennial topic in economics and political science (Eichengreen, 2012; Eichengreen, 2024; Helleiner and Kirshner, 2009; Kirshner, 2008; Norrlöf et al., 2020). While other currencies such as the Euro have gained importance for global transactions and for the storage of economic value, the dollar still dominates global commodity trade. This dominance has gained additional prominence due to the imposition of Western sanctions in the global payment system after the Russian attack on Ukraine (Nölke, 2022). The BRICS have highlighted their desire to encourage the use of their currencies instead of the dollar at the Johannesburg summit in August 2023. Our study complements existing studies on BRICS de-dollarization initiatives (Liu and Papa, 2022) by highlighting that we need to take a broader view on challenges to the liberal GFO, and that preparations for challenging the latter have progressed more widely than commonly perceived.

Importantly, however, our analysis of the BRICS' contestations of the liberal GFO's international dimension indicates that an alternative state-capitalist GFO does not contest the idea of international institutionalism in general. In some cases, the BRICS even demand to increase international coordination via international institutions, as in monetary policy. A superficial perspective only analyzing formal participation in global financial governance could even claim that BRICS generally are supportive of the existing international institutions (Larionova & Shelepov, 2022). The dividing line is rather on the exact design of international institutions.

First, the BRICS request more participation in international institutions as it was historically the case within the US-dominated Bretton Woods institutions. If the Western governments are not willing to provide this representation (to a sufficient degree), they set up alternative institutions, as observed in the field of development finance (NDB and AIIB) and balance-of-payment support (CRA). Some of the alternative institutions for a state-capitalist financial order are sponsored by the BRICS in total such as the CRA or NDB while others are not, such as alternative BITs or the creation of a multipolar currency system. Second, a major dividing line neither relates to the question of whether international institutions are needed or not nor to the power distribution within the existing institutions. It relates to the ideas guiding the operations of the international institutions of the GFO. Here the core difference with the liberal order is that state-capitalists demand (and design) far less intrusive international institutions. They clearly disagree with the idea of conditionalities – and they do not replace liberal conditionalities with state-capitalist conditionalities, if they set up alternative institutions (CRA, NDB and AIIB). Third, there is a major difference with regard to the public–private nature of international institutions of the GFO. Whereas the liberal order has a prominent role for transnational private governance (IASB, ISDS and rating agencies), the alternative state-capitalist order has a far more prominent role for intergovernmental cooperation, as, for instance, witnessed in the case of the public oversight of the IASB or the push for less private self-regulation through Basel III.

5.3 Limitations and Future Research Agenda

However, even our systematic approach still carries important limitations. A first case in point would be the incorporation of additional country cases. Although Anglo-America and the three Asian BRICS are at the center of the current contestation, it would be important to see how other advanced and emerging markets position themselves in this matter. There are substantial indications that many of these countries would mark some kind of middle ground between these poles. European economies like France, Italy or Germany may not fully share the liberal orientation of the leading Anglo-American economies with regard to the financial sector. Further, as Pape and Petry (2024) highlight, East Asian financial systems and actors from Korea, Taiwan and Japan are partially informed by developmental logics that share many similarities with state-capitalist principles. On the side of EMEs, it would also be interesting to see how other major emerging markets situate themselves in this continuum. Especially the relationship between EMEs, state capitalism and international financial hierarchies/subordination within the contemporary GFO requires further investigation (Alami et al., 2023).

This question is particularly important for Egypt, Ethiopia, Iran, Saudi Arabia and the UAE, the countries that were admitted to the BRICS grouping in January 2024. Especially the large financial systems of Saudi Arabia, UAE and Iran are much less liberal than in South Africa or Brazil and much closer to the more state-capitalist systems in India, Russia and China (Gray, 2020).[71] They have high degrees of state ownership, capital controls and state-led investment activities, boasting some of the largest SWFs and FX reserves globally (Montambault-Trudelle, 2023). This matters especially given their crucial role in global oil markets, which have until now been denominated in USD, having played a big role in the rise of the dollar as the de facto global currency (Spiro, 1999). After Iran switched to RMB-denominated oil trade with China early on due to sanctions, the recent moves to facilitate non-USD payments between China and UAE through the mBridge CBDC platform as well as Saudi Arabia's considerations of accepting yuan for oil trade with China point toward a potential shift or at least fragmentation of the global oil trade (also Mathews and Selden, 2018; McNally, 2020). This is not only limited to China as India and UAE agreed on paying for oil in rupees as well. How the BRICS expansion will further impact the contemporary GFO through issues like de-dollarization is thus an important area of future research.

One further limitation of our analysis is that while we have collected longer time-series of data for many issue areas, in order to cover eleven issue areas across seven countries, our analysis mostly focuses on current developments. A more comprehensive answer to the question of whether we are witnessing a major challenge to the liberal GFO would require more historical data in order to determine whether the degree of contestation is increasing or decreasing over the years. While our analysis partially illuminated this diachronic dimension, our main focus was on the synchronic comparison. Our systematic analysis could also be extended through conducting a series of in-depth case studies, ideally following a similar analytical approach. This would provide more nuance and empirical depth to the individual issue areas presented in this Element while maintaining the systematic character of our investigation. Better understanding these historical trajectories of GFO contestation is not only an important academic question but also has considerable practical and political implications. Wall Street, for example, certainly wants to know whether it can safely continue its current course with a major engagement within the Chinese financial sector or whether it might need a more cautions effort in the future as geopolitical tensions mount. Debates around splitting HSBC into a European and an Asian bank in 2022 are a case in point (Bloomberg News, 2022b).

Moreover, while we focus on the external contestation of the liberal GFO, this continuing external contestation may also lead to an increasing internal contestation, for example, as defensive measures in the context of an increasing

---

[71] With respect to the global financial system, Egypt and Ethiopia do not play an important role.

geopoliticization of finance (Petry, 2024). We have seen steps in this direction in which many Western governments implemented new screening mechanisms for FDI, particularly with regard to acquisitions by Chinese companies. We can observe a similar tendency of the liberal order self-undermining itself in the increased usage of financial sanctions as tools of economic statecraft in US–China power competition (Nölke, 2022; Weinhardt and Petry, 2024). The US has further started to weaponize finance for geopolitical reasons, both against Russia and China, thereby gradually undermining the liberal character of the contemporary GFO itself. These and other measures have led some observers to the argument that state capitalism is spreading in the power centers of the liberal order as well (van Apeldoorn and de Graaff, 2022), an argument that needs to be examined more systematically.

In a more general historical-dynamic comparison, it might be fruitful to compare the state-capitalist alternative to the GFO more systematically with the predecessor to neoliberalism, namely the multilateral "embedded liberalism" order that was prevalent in the three decades after World War II. When we apply the categories utilized in our study of the contemporary GFO to an ideal typical representation of finance under embedded liberalism, we note striking parallels. Both the post–World War II embedded GFO and the currently emerging state-capitalist alternative to the liberal GFO share many features that set them apart from the latter order. In both cases, the focus is on economic stability and on the protection of the domestic economy against major externally induced fluctuations. A general commitment toward the incremental process of economic liberalization combines with a high degree of control by national governments. The major difference between the embedded GFO and the state-capitalist GFO is that the latter takes place under financialization, whereas the former had strict controls of both domestic and trans-border financial flows. Still, governments supporting the state-capitalist model have learned to combine a high degree of financialization with a high degree of state control (Petry et al., 2021b).

Another important avenue of future research is whether the substantial (state-capitalist) challenge emanating from Russia, India and China potentially also extends beyond finance, as could be observed in what seems like a growing economic and political alignment after Russia's invasion of Ukraine. While many observers expected China to side with Russia, India's stance took many pundits by surprise. Of course, an important open question remains as to how far this is a conscious, collective and coordinated challenge, or rather an uneasy constellation that emerged as a result of geostrategic necessities. In any case, we can observe striking similarities between these countries' behaviors beyond finance – be it abstentions from UN resolutions that condemned Russia's attack on Ukraine or creating innovative ways to boost bilateral trade despite Western sanctions. Together, China, India and Russia constitute what could tentatively be called "emerging Asia's state-capitalist challenge" to the liberal GFO, maybe even to economic liberalism more generally. We therefore argue that future research should place greater focus on the Russia–India–China constellation and how their state-capitalist economic models intersect with other issue areas such as security, technology or geopolitics.

The liberal GFO still dominates global finance and has not been replaced by a state-capitalist alternative. We can, however, observe cracks emerging in what used to be a hegemonic project (in the Gramscian sense; Bates, 1975). The BRICS, especially China, India and Russia, have achieved significant levels of autonomy, resisting pressures to conform with liberal norms and to accept power constellations inherent in the contemporary GFO, and even creating alternative spaces both in other countries and by forming global institutions that follow decidedly state-capitalist principles. The geopolitical turn will likely exacerbate this development. While the center of gravity in the global economy is gradually shifting East, more attention needs to be paid to these global realignments, contestations and these new worlds in which global financial transactions are increasingly being shaped.

References

Abdelal, R. (2007). *Capital rules: The construction of global finance*. Ithaca: Cornell University Press.

Adler-Nissen, R. & Zarakol, A. (2021). Struggles for recognition: The liberal international order and the merger of its discontents. *International Organization*, 75(2), 611–634.

AidData. (2021). *Banking on the Belt and Road: Insights from a new global dataset of 13,427 Chinese development projects*. Williamsburg: AidData at William & Mary.

Alami, I. & Dixon, A. (2020). State capitalism(s) redux? Theories, tensions, controversies. *Competition & Change*, 24(1), 70–94.

Alami, I. (2020). *Money power and financial capital in emerging markets: Facing the liquidity tsunami*. London: Routledge.

Alami, I., Alves, C., Bonizzi, B. et al. (2023). International financial subordination: A critical research agenda. *Review of International Political Economy*, 30(4), 1360–1386.

Allen, F. & Gale, D. (2000). *Comparing financial systems*. Cambridge, MA: MIT Press.

van Apeldoorn, B. & de Graaff, N. (2022). The state in global capitalism before and after the covid-19 crisis. *Contemporary Politics*, 28(3), 306–327.

Armijo, L. & Katada, S. (eds.) (2014). *The financial statecraft of emerging powers: Shield and sword in Asia and Latin America*. New York: Springer.

Asmus, G., Fuchs, A. & Müller, A. (2017). *BRICS and foreign aid*. AidData, Working Paper, No. 43. www.aiddata.org/publications/brics-and-foreign-aid.

Asmus, G., Eichenauer, V. Z., Fuchs, A. & Parks, B. (2021). *Does India use development finance to compete with China? A subnational analysis*. Kiel Institute for the World Economy, No. 2189.

Authers, J. (2018). *Indices don't just measure markets – They drive performance*. Financial Times, June 23.

Ayres, J., Garcia, M., Guillén, D. A. & Kehoe, P. J. (2019). *The monetary and fiscal history of Brazil, 1960–2016*. National Bureau of Economic Research, No. 25421.

Babic, M., Garcia-Bernardo, J. & Heemskerk, E. M. (2020). The rise of transnational state capital: State-led foreign investment in the 21st century. *Review of International Political Economy*, 27(3), 433–475.

Baker, A., Hudson, D. & Woodward, R. (2005). *Governing financial globalization: International political economy and multi-level governance*. London: Routledge.

Ban, C. & Blyth, M. (2013). The BRICS and the Washington consensus: An introduction. *Review of International Political Economy*, 20(2), 241–255.

Barma, N., Ratner, E. & Weber, S. (2007). A world without the West. *The National Interest*, 90, 23–30.

Barone, B. & Spratt, S. (2015). *Rising powers in international development: Development banks from the BRICS*. Institute of Development Studies, Evidence Report, No. 111.

Bates, T. R. (1975). Gramsci and the Theory of Hegemony. *Journal of the History of Ideas*, 36(2), 351–366.

Batista, P. N. (2022). *The BRICS and the financing mechanisms they created: Progress and shortcomings*. London: Anthem Press.

Beattie, A. (2012). *IMF drops opposition to capital controls*. Financial Times, December 3.

Beausang, F. (2012). *Globalization and the BRICs: Why the BRICs will not rule the world for long*. New York: Springer.

BIS. (2019). *Statistical release: OTC derivatives statistics at end-June 2019*. Bank for International Settlement.

Bismuth, R. (2017). The "Santiago Principles" for sovereign wealth funds: The shortcomings and the futility of self-regulation. *European Business Law Review*, 28(1), 69–88.

Bloomberg News. (2022a). *Sanctions on Russia puts focus on China's central bank*. Bloomberg, February 28. www.bloomberg.com/news/articles/2022-02-28/sanctions-on-russia-puts-focus-on-china-s-central-bank.

Bloomberg News. (2022b). *Britain's biggest bank is caught in the U.S.-China crossfire*. Bloomberg, May 8.

Blyth, M. (2012). *Great transformations: Economic ideas and institutional change in the twentieth century*. Cambridge: Cambridge University Press.

Bond, P. (2016). BRICS banking and the debate over sub-imperialism. *Third World Quarterly*, 37(4), 611–629.

Börzel, T. A. & Zürn, M. (2021). Contestations of the liberal international order: From liberal multilateralism to postnational liberalism. *International Organization*, 75(2), 282–305.

Bonizzi, B. & Kaltenbrunner, A. (2018). Liability-driven investment and pension fund exposure to emerging markets: A Minskyan analysis. *Environment and Planning A: Economy and Space*, 51(2), 420–439.

Bonizzi, B., Kaltenbrunner, A. & Powell, J. (2022). Financialised capitalism and the subordination of emerging capitalist economies. *Cambridge Journal of Economics*, 46(4), 651–678.

Bräutigam, D. (2011). Aid "with Chinese characteristics": Chinese foreign aid and development finance meet the OECD-DAC aid regime. *Journal of International Development*, 23(5), 752–764.

Braun, B. & Koddenbrock, K. (2021). *Capital claims: Following finance across borders*. London: Routledge.

Braw, E. (2023). *New Russian Law takes corporate hostages*. Foreign Policy, September 1.

Bretton Woods Project. (2011). Brazil, India spurn IMF capital controls framework. Bretton Woods Project, 25 June.

Bretton Woods Project. (2014). *Brazil, India spurn IMF capital controls framework*. Bretton Woods Project, January 28.

Broz, J. L., Frieden, J. & Weymouth, S. (2021). Populism in place: The economic geography of the globalization backlash. *International Organization*, 75(2), 64–494.

Ca'Zorzi, M., Dedola, L., Georgiadis, G. et al. (2020). *Monetary policy and its transmission in a globalised world*. ECB, Working paper, No. 2407.

Camfferman, K. (2020). International accounting standard setting and geopolitics. *Accounting in Europe*, 17(3), 243–263.

Cammack, P. (2018). Situating the Asian Infrastructure Investment Bank in the context of global economic governance. *Journal of Chinese Economic and Business Studies*, 16(3), 241–258.

Cattaneo, N., Biziwick, M. & Fryer, D. (2015). *The BRICS Contingent Reserve Arrangement and its position in the emerging global financial architecture*. SAIIA Policy Insights, No. 10.

Cerutti, E., Koch, C. & Pradhan, S. K. (2020). *Banking across borders: Are Chinese banks different?* Bank for International Settlement (BIS), Working Paper, No. 892.

Chadda, N. K. & Vardia, S. (2020). Fair value accounting and valuation of non-financial assets: A study of impact of IFRS adoption. *Journal of Commerce & Accounting Research*, 9(4), 63–72.

Chen, H. (2019). Reforming ISDS: A Chinese perspective. In Y. Li, T. Qi and C. Bian, eds., *China, the EU and International Investment Law*. London: Routledge, 100–111.

Chijioke-Oforji, C. (2019). *Assessing the effectiveness of sovereign wealth fund governance and regulation through the Santiago principles and the International Forum of Sovereign Wealth Funds*. Unpublished Doctoral thesis.

Chin, G. T. (2014). The BRICS-led development bank: Purpose and politics beyond the G20. *Global Policy*, 5(3), 366–373.

Chin, G. T. & Gallagher, K. P. (2019). Coordinated credit spaces: The globalization of Chinese development finance. *Development and Change*, 50(1), 245–274.

Chinn, M. D., & Ito, H. (2006). What matters for financial development? Capital controls, institutions, and interactions. *Journal of Development Economics*, 81(1), 163–192.

Chwieroth, J. M. (2010). *Capital ideas: The IMF and the rise of financial liberalization*. Princeton: Princeton University Press.

Clarida, R. H. (2021). *Perspectives on global monetary policy coordination, cooperation, and correlation*. Federal Reserve, November 19.

Cohen, B. J. (2012). The Yuan tomorrow? Evaluating China's currency internationalisation strategy. *New Political Economy*, 17(3), 361–371.

Cohen, B. J. (2019). *Currency statecraft: Monetary rivalry and geopolitical ambition*. Chicago: The University of Chicago Press.

Combs, A., Samy, M. & Myachina, A. (2013). Cultural impact of the harmonization of Russian accounting standards with the International Financial Reporting Standards: A practitioner's perspective. *Journal of Accounting & Organizational Change*, 9(1), 26–49.

Cormier, B. & Naqvi, N. (2023). Delegating discipline: How indexes restructured the political economy of sovereign bond markets. *The Journal of Politics*, 85(4), 1501–1515.

Creutz, K. (2023). The Asian Infrastructure Investment Bank (AIIB) and rights protection: Revisionist or just another kid on the block? *The International Journal of Human Rights*, 27(7), 1107–1132.

Dafe, F. & Williams, Z. (2021). Banking on courts: Financialization and the rise of third-party funding in investment arbitration. *Review of International Political Economy*, 28(5), 1362–1384.

Das, M. S. (2019). *China's evolving exchange rate regime*. International Monetary Fund, Working Paper, No. 2019/050.

Davis, J. S., Fujiwara, I., Huang, K. X. D. & Wang, J. (2022). *Russia counters sanctions' impact with currency controls, averts crisis (for now)*. Federal Reserve Bank of Dallas, May 31.

De Conti, B. & Diegues, A. C. (2022). Foreign direct investments in the BRICS countries and internationalization of Chinese capital. *BRICS Journal of Economics*, 3(3), 129–142.

de Graaff, N., ten Brink, T. & Parmar, I. (2020). China's rise in a liberal world order in transition. *Review of International Political Economy*, 27(2), 191–207.

Deng, Q., Xiao, W. & Yan, H. (2022). The spillover effects of U.S. monetary policy normalization on the BRICS based on panel VAR model. *Journal of Mathematics*, 2022, 1–9.

Dierckx, S. (2013). After the crisis and beyond the new constitutionalism? The case of the free movement of capital. *Globalizations*, 10(6), 803–818.

Dierckx, S. (2015). China's capital controls: Between contender state and integration into the heartland. *International Politics*, 52(6), 724–742.

Dreher, A., Fuchs, A. & Nunnenkamp, P. (2013). New donors. *International Interactions*, 39(3), 402–415.

Drezner, D. W. & McNamara, K. R. (2013). International political economy, global financial orders and the 2008 financial crisis. *Perspectives on Politics*, 11(1), 155–166.

Dua, P. & Ranjan, R. (2012). *Exchange rate policy and modelling in India*. OUP Catalogue.

EBA. (2022). *Report on EU dependence on non-EU banks and on funding in foreign currency*. Brussels: European Banking Authority.

The Economist. (2022). *China does not always collect its debts on time*. The Economist, February 10.

Eichengreen, B. (2012). *Exorbitant privilege: The rise and fall of the dollar and the future of the international monetary system*. Oxford: Oxford University Press.

Eichengreen, B. (2024). International finance and geopolitics. *Asian Economic Policy Review*, *19*(1), 84–100.

Engel, C. (2016). International coordination of central bank policy. *Journal of International Money and Finance*, 67, 13–25.

Epstein, G. A. (2005). Introduction: Financialization and the world economy. In G. A. Epstein, ed., *Financialization and the World Economy*. Cheltenham: Edward Elgar, pp. 3–16.

Farrell, H. & Newman, A. L. (2014). Domestic institutions beyond the nation-state: Charting the new interdependence approach. *World Politics*, 66(2), 331–363.

Farrell, H. & Newman, A. L. (2021). The Janus face of the liberal international information order: When global institutions are self-undermining. *International Organization*, 75(2), 333–358.

Feldmann, M. (2019). Global varieties of capitalism. *World Politics*, 71(1), 162–196.

Fichtner, J. (2017). Perpetual decline or persistent dominance? Uncovering Anglo-America's true structural power in global finance. *Review of International Studies*, 43(1), 3–28.

Fichtner, J., Heemskerk, E. M., & Petry, J. (2022). The new gatekeepers of financial claims: States, passive markets, and the growing power of index providers. In B. Braun & K. Koddenbrock, eds., *Capital claims: Following finance across borders*. London: Routledge, pp.107–129.

Flaherty, T. M. & Rogowski, R. (2021). Rising inequality as a threat to the liberal international order. *International Organization*, 75(2), 495–523.

FSDC. (2019). *Hong Kong builds on offshore RMB connections.* Forbes, November 15.

Gallagher, Kevin P. (2015). Ruling Capital Emerging Markets and the Reregulation of Cross-Border Finance. Cornell: Cornell University Press.

Gabor, D. (2021). The wall street consensus. *Development and Change*, 52(3), 429–459.

Grabel, I. (2017). *When things don't fall apart: Global financial governance and developmental finance in an age of productive incoherence.* Cambridge: MIT Press.

Gehlenborg, N. & Wong, B. (2012). Heat maps. *Nature Methods*, 9(3), 213.

Gelpern, A., Horn, S., Morris, S., Parks, B. & Trebesch, C. (2022). *How China lends: A rare look into 100 debt contracts with foreign governments.* Washington, DC: Peterson Institute for International Economics.

Germain, R. (2009). Financial order and world politics: Crisis, change and continuity. *International Affairs*, 85(4), 669–687.

Germain, R. (2010). *Global politics and financial governance.* Basingstoke: Palgrave Macmillan.

Global Times. (2023). *Over 80% of Russia-China trade settlement now using local currencies: Russian president.* Global Times, June 17.

Goddard, S. E., Krebs, R. R., Kreuder-Sonnen, C. & Rittberger, B. (2024) Contestation in a world of liberal orders. *Global Studies Quarterly.* www .researchgate.net/publication/374949620_Contestation_in_a_world_of_liberal_ orders.

Goldman, D. P. (2022). *India-Russia currency swaps bypass US sanctions.* Asia Times, March 28.

Goldstein, J. & Gulotty, R. (2021). America and the trade regime: What went wrong? *International Organization*, 55(4), 524–557.

Gourinchas, P.-O., Rey, H. & Sauzet, M. (2019). The international monetary and financial system. *Annual Review of Economics*, 11(1), 859–893.

Graeber, D. (2011). *Debt: The first 5,000 years.* New York: Melville House.

Gray, J. (2020). Treaty shopping and unintended consequences: BRICS in the international system. In S. Y. Kim, ed., *BRICS and the Global Economy*, Singapore: World Press, 259–285.

Gray, M. (2018). *The economy of the gulf states.* Newcastle upon Tyne: Agenda.

Green, J. (2020). *The political economy of the special relationship: Anglo-American development from the gold standard to the financial crisis.* Princeton: Princeton University Press.

Griffith-Jones, S. (2014). *A BRICS development bank: A dream coming true?* United Nations Conference on Trade and Development (UNCTAD), Discussion Papers, No. 215.

Gruin, J., Knaack, P. & Xu, J. (2018). Tailoring for development: China's Postcrisis influence in global financial governance. *Global Policy*, 9(4), 467–478.

Hall, P. A. & Soskice, D. (eds.) (2001). *Varieties of capitalism: The institutional foundations of comparative advantage.* Oxford: Oxford University Press.

Hameiri, S. & Jones, L. (2018). China challenges global governance? Chinese international development finance and the AIIB. *International Affairs*, 94(3), 573–593.

Hancock, T. & Cohen, M. (2023). *How BRICS became a club that others want to join.* Bloomberg, November 3.

Helleiner, E. (1995). Explaining the globalization of financial markets: Bringing states back in. *Review of International Political Economy*, 2(2), 315–341.

Helleiner, E. (1996). *States and the reemergence of global finance: From bretton woods to the 1990s.* Ithaca: Cornell University Press.

Helleiner, E. (2014). *The status quo crisis: Global financial governance after the 2008 meltdown.* Oxford: Oxford University Press.

Helleiner, E. & Kirschner, J. (2014). *The great wall of money: Power and politics in China's international monetary relations.* Ithaca: Cornell University Press.

Helleiner, E. & Kirshner, J. (eds.) (2009). *The future of the dollar.* Ithaca: Cornell University Press.

Helleiner, E., Pagliari, S. & Zimmermann, H. (2010). *Global finance in crisis: The politics of international regulatory change.* London: Routledge.

Helleiner, E. & Wang, H. (2018). Limits to the BRICS' challenge: Credit rating reform and institutional innovation in global finance. *Review of International Political Economy*, 25(5), 573–595.

Henning, C. R. & Walter, A. (eds.) (2016). *Global financial governance confronts emerging powers.* Waterloo: Centre for International Governance Innovation.

Hernandez, D. (2017). Are "new" donors challenging world bank conditionality? *World Development*, 96, 529–549.

Holtbrügge, D. & Kreppel, H. (2012). Determinants of outward foreign direct investment from BRIC countries: An explorative study. *International Journal of Emerging Markets*, 7(1), 4–30.

Hooijmaaijers, B. (2021). The internal and external institutionalization of the BRICS countries: The case of the New Development Bank. *International Political Science Review*, 43(4), 481–494.

Horch, D. & Popper, N. (2013). *Despite Risks, Brazil Courts the Millisecond Investor*. NYT DealBook, May 24.

Horn, S., Reinhart, C. M. & Trebesch, C. (2022). *Hidden defaults*. Kiel, Working Paper, No. 2208.

Huotari, M. & Hanemann, T. (2014). Emerging powers and change in the global financial order. *Global Policy*, 5(3), 298–310.

IFRS. (2022). *Who uses IFRS Accounting Standards?* Retrieved February 12, 2023, www.ifrs.org/use-around-the-world/use-of-ifrs-standards-by-jurisdiction/.

IMF. (2012). *Liberalizing capital flows and managing outflows – background paper*. Washington, DC: International Monetary Fund.

IMF. (2018). *Reserve currency blocs: A changing international monetary system?* Washington, DC: International Monetary Fund.

IMF. (2021). *Annual report on exchange arrangements and exchange restrictions 2020*. Washington, DC: International Monetary Fund.

ING. (2020). *Russian de-dollarisation Public-private divergence persists*. ING Research, December 3.

Islam, M. S. (2022). *Western "China debt trap" propaganda a geopolitical tool, deliberately confusing truth*. Global Times, August 17.

Jackson, G. & Deeg, R. (2008). From comparing capitalisms to the politics of institutional change. *Review of International Political Economy*, 15(4), 680–709.

Jiamai, W. (2022). *India's rupee settlement echoes global de-dollarization push*. Global Times, July 12.

Jiang, W. (2009). Fueling the dragon: China's rise and its energy and resources extraction in Africa. *The China Quarterly*, 199, 585–609.

Johnson, J. (2004). *Does central bank independence matter in Russia?* PONARS, Policy Memo, No. 349.

Jones, E. (2022). The politics of regulatory convergence and divergence. In E. Jones, ed., *The political economy of bank regulation in developing countries*. Oxford: Oxford University Press, pp. 68–103.

Jones, E. & Zeitz, A. O. (2017). The limits of globalizing Basel banking standards. *Journal of Financial Regulation*, 3(1), 89–124.

Kalinowski, T. (2013). Regulating international finance and the diversity of capitalism. *Socio-Economic Review*, 11(3), 471–496.

Kaplan, S. B. (2021). *Globalizing patient capital: The political economy of Chinese finance in the Americas*. Cambridge: Cambridge University Press.

Karwowski, E., Shabani, M., & Stockhammer, E. (2020). Dimensions and determinants of financialisation: Comparing OECD countries since 1997. *New Political Economy*, 25(6), 957–977.

Kirshner, J. (1999). Keynes, capital mobility and the crisis of embedded liberalism. *Review of International Political Economy*, 6(3), 313–337.

Kirshner, J. (2008). Dollar primacy and American power: What's at stake? *Review of International Political Economy*, 15(3), 418–438.

Konings, M. (2007). The institutional foundations of US structural power in international finance: From the re-emergence of global finance to the monetarist turn. *Review of International Political Economy*, 15(1), 35–61.

Konings, M. (2016). Governing the system: Risk, finance, and neoliberal reason. *European Journal of International Relations*, 22(2), 268–288.

Kring, W. N. & Gallagher, K. P. (2019). Strengthening the Foundations? Alternative Institutions for Finance and Development. *Development and Change*, 50(1), 3–23.

Kurlantzick, J. (2016). *State capitalism: How the return of statism is transforming the world*. Oxford: Oxford University Press.

Lake, D. A., Martin, L. L. & Risse, T. (2021). Challenges to the liberal order: Reflections on international organization. *International Organization*, 75(2), 225–257.

Lall, R. (2010). Reforming global banking rules: Back to the future? Danish Institute for International Studies (DIIS), Copenhagen, DIIS Working Paper No. 2010:16.

Langley, P. (2003). *World financial orders: An historical international political economy*. London: Routledge.

Larionova, M. & Shelepov, A. (2022). BRICS, G20 and global economic governance reform. *International Political Science Review*, 43(4), 512–530.

Lauria, V. & Fumagalli, C. (2019). BRICS, the southern model, and the evolving landscape of development assistance: Toward a new taxonomy. *Public Administration and Development*, 39(4–5), 215–230.

Lazonick, W. & O'Sullivan, M. (2000). Maximizing shareholder value: A new ideology for corporate governance. *Economy & Society*, 29(1), 13–35.

Li, Y.-W. V. (2018). *China's financial opening: Coalition politics and policy changes*. London: Routledge.

Liu, I. T. & Dixon, A. D. (2021). Legitimating state capital: The global financial professions and the transnationalization of Chinese sovereign wealth. *Development and Change*, 52(5), 1251–1273.

Liu, H., & Lim, G. (2023). When the state goes transnational: The political economy of China's engagement with indonesia. *Competition & Change*, 27(2), 402–421.

Liu, Z. Z. & Papa, M. (2022). *Can BRICS de-dollarize the global financial system?* Cambridge: Cambridge University Press.

Lockett, H. & Hale, T. (2020). *Global investors place RMB1tn bet on China breakthrough*. Financial Times, December 14.

Logvinenko, I. O. (2021). *Global finance, local control: Corruption and wealth in contemporary Russia*. Ithaca: Cornell University Press.

Lu, Marcu. (2023). *Visualizing the BRICS Expansion in 4 Charts*. Visual Capitalist, August 24.

MacKenzie, D., Beunza, D., Millo, Y. & Pardo-Guerra, J. P. (2012). Drilling through the Allegheny Mountains: Liquidity, materiality and high-frequency trading. *Journal of Cultural Economy*, 5(3), 279–296.

Madan, L. (2015). *Unlocking HFT at the Moscow Exchange: What the numbers say?* Finance Magnates, July 30.

Mansfield, E. D. & Rudra, N. (2021). Embedded liberalism in the digital era. *International Organization*, 75(2), 558–585.

Mathews, J. A. & Selden, M. (2018). China: The emergence of the petroyuan and the challenge to US dollar hegemony. *The Asia-Pacific Journal*, 16(22/3), 1–12.

Mattli, W. (2019). *Darkness by design: The hidden power in global capital markets*. Princeton: Princeton University Press.

McDowell, D. (2016). *Brother, can you spare a billion? The United States, the IMF, and the international lender of last resort*. Oxford: Oxford University Press.

McDowell, D. (2023). *Bucking the buck: US financial sanctions and the international backlash against the dollar*. Oxford: Oxford University Press.

McNally, C. A. (2020). Chaotic mélange: Neo-liberalism and neo-statism in the age of Sino-capitalism. *Review of International Political Economy*, 27(2), 281–301.

McNally, C. A. & Gruin, J. (2017). A novel pathway to power? Contestation and adaptation in China's internationalization of the RMB. *Review of International Political Economy*, 24(4), 599–628.

Mearsheimer, J. J. (2019). Bound to fail: The rise and fall of the liberal international order. *International Security*, 43(4), 7–50.

Mellow, C. (2014). *High frequency trading gets a mixed reception in emerging markets*. Institutional Investor, June 9.

Mertens, D., Thiemann, M. & Volberding, P. (2021). *The reinvention of development banking in the European Union: Industrial policy in the single market and the emergence of a field*. Oxford: Oxford University Press.

Meyer, D. R. & Guernsey, G. (2015). Global exchanges in the HFT nexus. In G. N. Gregoriou, ed., *The handbook of high frequency trading*. San Diego: Academic Press, pp. 171–194.

Mitchell, C. (2022). *"Chinese banks want to be repaid in full": Skepticism greets China's debt forgiveness*. African Business, September 26.

Mminele, D. (2013). *Note on the foreign exchange market operations of the South African Reserve Bank*. BIS Paper, No. 73.

Mohan, R. & Kapur, M. (2019). *Monetary policy coordination and the role of central banks*. IMF, Working Paper, No. 14/70.

Montambault-Trudelle, A. (2023). The public investment fund and Salman's state: The political drivers of sovereign wealth management in Saudi Arabia. *Review of International Political Economy*, 30(2), 747–771.

Moraes, H. C. & Hees, F. (2018). Breaking the BIT Mold: Brazil's pioneering approach to investment agreements. *American Journal of International Law*, 112, 197–201.

Moramudali, U. (2019). *Is Sri Lanka really a victim of China's "debt trap"?* The Diplomat, May 14.

Moramudali, U. (2020). *The Hambantota port deal: Myths and realities*. The Diplomat, January 1.

Moschella, M. & Tsingou, E. (2013). Conclusions: Too little, too slow. In M. Moschella and E. Tsingou, eds., *Great expectations, slow transformations: Incremental change in post-crisis regulation*. Essex: ECPR Press, pp. 193–215.

MSCI. (2010). *Global market accessibility review 2010*. MSCI. June.

MSCI. (2018a). *MSCI market classification framework: Consultation on potential methodology enhancements*. MSCI. June.

MSCI. (2018b). *New anti-competitive measures impacting the Indian equity market*. MSCI. February.

MSCI. (2020). *Global market accessibility review 2020*. MSCI. June.

MSCI. (2021). *Global market accessibility review 2021*. MSCI. June.

MSCI. (2022). *Global market accessibility review 2022*. MSCI. June.

MSCI. (2023). *Global market accessibility review 2023*. MSCI. June.

Musacchio, A. & Lazzarini, S. G. (2013). *Reinventing state capitalism: Leviathan in business, Brazil and beyond*. Cambridge: Harvard University Press.

Narayan, K. (2021). *The NSE co-location case investigation, and what SEBI's new order means*. Indian Express, February 12.

Nasdaq. (2021). *Totalmarkets: Blueprint for a better tomorrow*. Nasdaq White Paper, April.

Naughton, B. & Tsai, K. S. (2015). *State capitalism, institutional adaptation and the Chinese miracle*. Cambridge: Cambridge University Press.

Nölke, A. (2010). The politics of accounting regulation. In E. Helleiner, S. Pagliari and H. Zimmermann, eds., *Global finance in crisis: The politics of international regulatory change*. London: Routledge, 37–55.

Nölke, A. (2011). *Transnational economic order and national economic institutions: Comparative capitalism meets international political economy.* Max Planck Institute for the Study of Societies, MPIfG, Working Paper, No. 11/13.

Nölke, A. (2015a). International financial regulation and domestic coalitions in state-permeated capitalism: China and global banking rules. *International Politics,* 52(6), 743–759.

Nölke, A. (2015b). Rising powers and transnational private governance: The International Accounting Standards Board. In D. Lesage and T. Graaf, eds., *Rising powers and multilateral institutions.* New York: Springer, pp. 96–116.

Nölke, A. (2022). Geoeconomic infrastructures: Building Chinese-Russian alternatives to swift. In B. Braun and K. Koddenbrock, eds., *Capital claims.* London: Routledge, pp. 147–166.

Nölke, A. (2023). *Second image IPE: Bridging the gap between comparative and international political economy.* London: Palgrave.

Nölke, A. & Perry, J. (2007a). Coordination service firms and the erosion of Rhenish capitalism. In H. Overbeek, B. van Apeldoorn and A. Nölke, eds., *The transnational politics of corporate governance regulation.* London: Routledge, pp. 121–140.

Nölke, A. & Perry, J. (2007b). The power of transnational private governance: Financialization and the IASB. *Business and Politics,* 9(3), 1–25.

Nölke, A., ten Brink, T., May, C., & Claar, S. (2020). *State-permeated capitalism in large emerging economies.* London: Routledge.

Norrlöf, C., Poast, P., Cohen, B. J. et al. (2020). Global monetary order and the liberal order debate. *International Studies Perspectives,* 21(2), 109–153.

Oatley, T., Winecoff, W. K., Pennock, A., & Bauerle Danzman, S. (2013). The political economy of global finance: A network model. *Perspectives on Politics,* 11(1), 133–153.

Ocampo, J. A. (2017). *Resetting the international monetary (non) system.* Oxford: Oxford University Press

OECD. (2019). *Owners of the world's listed companies.* Paris: OECD.

OECD. (2020). *Multilateral development finance 2020.* Paris: OECD.

OECD. (2021). *Liberalization of capital movements.* Paris: OECD.

Öniş, Z. & Kutlay, M. (2020). The new age of hybridity and clash of norms: China, BRICS, and challenges of global governance in a postliberal global order. *Alternatives: Global, Local, Political,* 45(3), 123–142.

Pandya, A., van Zijl, W. & Maroun, W. (2021). Fair value accounting implementation challenges in South Africa. *Journal of Accounting in Emerging Economies,* 11(2), 216–246 .

Pape, F. (2022). Governing global liquidity: Federal reserve swap lines and the international dimension of US monetary policy. *New Political Economy*, 27(3), 455–472 .

Pape, F. & Petry, J. (2024). East Asia and the politics of global finance: A developmental challenge to the neoliberal consensus? *Review of International Political Economy*, 31(1), 224–252.

Parameswaran, P. (2010). *China's global profile increases with key IMF post.* The Sydney Morning Herald, February 25.

Paul, T. V. (2021). Globalization, deglobalization and reglobalization: Adapting liberal international order. *International Affairs*, 97(5), 1599–1620.

Peng, S. & Bewley, K. (2010). Adaptability to fair value accounting in an emerging economy: A case study of China's IFRS convergence. *Accounting, Auditing & Accountability Journal*, 23(8), 982–1011.

Perks, M., Rao, Y., Shin, M. J. & Tokuoka, K. (2021). *Evolution of bilateral swap lines*. IMF, Working Paper, No. WP/21/210.

Perry, J. & Nölke, A. (2006). The political economy of international accounting standards. *Review of International Political Economy*, 13(4), 559–586.

Petry, J. (2020). Financialization with Chinese characteristics? Exchanges, control and capital markets in authoritarian capitalism. *Economy & Society*, 49(2), 213–238.

Petry, J. (2021a). From national marketplaces to global providers of financial infrastructures: Exchanges, infrastructures and structural power in global finance. *New Political Economy*, 26(4), 574–597.

Petry, J. (2021b). Same same, but different: Varieties of capital markets, Chinese state capitalism and the global financial order. *Competition & Change*, 25(5), 605–630.

Petry, J. (2023). Beyond ports, roads and railways: Chinese statecraft, the Belt and Road initiative and the politics of financial infrastructures. *European Journal of International Relations*, 29(2), 319–351.

Petry, J. (2024). China's rise, weaponized interdependence and the increasingly contested geographies of global finance.*Finance & Space*, 1(1), 49–57.

Petry, J., Fichtner, J. & Heemskerk, E. M. (2021). Steering capital: The growing private authority of index providers in the age of passive asset management. *Review of International Political Economy*, 28(1), 152–176.

Petry, J., Koddenbrock, K. & Nölke, A. (2023). State capitalism and capital markets: Comparing securities exchanges in emerging markets. *Environment and Planning A*, 55(1), 143–164.

Porter, T. (2005). *Globalization and finance*. London: Polity.

Potin, N. & De Urquiza, C. B. (2021). *The Brazilian cooperation and facilitation investment agreement: Are foreign investors protected?* Kluwer Arbitration Blog, December 28.

Qing, K. G. (2015). *Exclusive: China's AIIB to offer loans with fewer strings attached*. Reuters, September 2.

Raess, D., Ren, W. & Wagner, P. (2017). *Chinese commercially-oriented financial flows and UN voting realignment*. (Unpublished manuscript). www.peio.me/wp-content/uploads/2018/01/PEIO11_paper_62.pdf.

Rakshit, T. K. (2017). Spillover effect of unconventional monetary policy and international monetary policy coordination. *Journal of Applied Business and Economics*, 19(7), 84–98.

Ramanna, K. (2013). The international politics of IFRS harmonization. *Accounting Economics and Law: A Convivium*, 3(2), 1–46.

Ranjan, P., Singh, H. V., James, K. & Singh, R. (2018). *India's model bilateral investment treaty: Is India too risk averse?* Brookings India IMPACT Series, No. 082018.

RBI. (2013). *Operation and performance of commercial banks*. Reserve Bank of India, November 12.

Reuters. (2009). *China, India, Brazil join inner regulatory circle*. February 19.

Reuters. (2017). *China doles out $100 million punishment to Russian-controlled fund for role in 2015 crash*. June 24.

Reuters. (2022). *China-led SCO bloc agrees to expand trade in national currencies*. September 16.

Roberts, A., Moraes H. C. & Ferguson, V. (2019). Toward a geoeconomic order in international trade and investment. *Journal of International Economic Law*, 22, 655–676.

Roberts, C. A., Armijo, L. E. & Katada, S. N. (2018). *The BRICS and collective financial statecraft*. Oxford: Oxford University Press.

Ruggie, J. G. (1982). International regimes, transactions, and change: Embedded liberalism in the postwar economic order. *International Organization*, 36(2), 379–415.

Samples, T. R. (2019). Winning and losing in investor–state dispute settlement. *American Business Law Journal*, 56(1), 115–175.

Schapiro, M. G. (2024). Prudential developmentalism: Explaining the combination of the developmental state and Basel rules in Brazilian banking regulation. *Regulation & Governance*. https://onlinelibrary.wiley.com/doi/abs/10.1111/rego.12389.

Silva, A. P., Fontes, A. & Martins, A. (2021). Perceptions regarding the implementation of international financial reporting standards in Portugal and Brazil. *Journal of International Accounting, Auditing and Taxation*, 44, 1–18.

Simes, D. (2020). *China and Russia ditch dollar in move toward "financial alliance"*. Nikkei Asian Review, August 6.

Simmons, B. A. (2014). Bargaining over bits, arbitrating awards: The regime for protection and promotion of international investment. *World Politics*, 66(1), 12–46.

Simmons, B. A., & Goemans H. E. (2021). Built on borders: Tensions with the institution liberalism (thought it) left behind. *International Organization*, 75(2), 387–410.

Sohn, I. (2013). Between confrontation and assimilation: China and the fragmentation of global financial governance. *Journal of Contemporary China*, 22(82), 630–648.

Spiro, D. E. (1999). *The hidden hand of American hegemony: Petrodollar recycling and international markets*. Ithaca: Cornell University Press.

Stone, R. W., Wang, Y. & Yu, S. (2022). Chinese power and the state-owned enterprise. *International Organization*, 76(1), 229–250.

Stuenkel, O. (2020). *The BRICS and the future of global order* (2nd ed.). London: Lexington Books.

Subacchi, P. (2018). *The people's money: How China is building a global currency*. New York: Columbia University Press.

SWFI. (2023). *Top 51 largest development bank rankings by total assets*. SWFI. Retrieved November 9, 2023, www.swfinstitute.org/fund-rankings/development-bank.

Tan, A. & Robertson, B. (2018). *MSCI weighs capping India, Brazil weights over investor access*. Bloomberg, May 30.

ten Brink, T. (2015). Chinese firms "going global": Recent OFDI trends, policy support and international implications. *International Politics*, 52(6), 666–683.

Tian, H. (2016). The BRICS and the G20. *China & World Economy*, 24(4), 111–126.

Vernikov, A. V. (2015). Comparing the banking models in China and Russia: Revisited. *Studies on Russian Economic Development*, 26(2), 178–187.

Vernikov, A. V. (2017). *The impact of state-controlled banks on the Russian banking sector*. MPRA, Paper, No. 77155.

Viktorov, I. & Abramov, A. (2016). The state capture of Russian non-bank financial institutions and markets after the 2008 crisis. *Competition & Change*, 20(1), 3–20.

Wang, H. (2017). New multilateral development banks: Opportunities and challenges for global governance. *Global Policy*, 8(1), 113–118.

Wang, H. (2019). The New Development Bank and the Asian Infrastructure Investment Bank: China's ambiguous approach to global financial governance. *Development and Change*, 50(1), 221–244.

Weghmann, V. & Hall, D. (2021). The unsustainable political economy of investor–state dispute settlement mechanisms. *International Review of Administrative Sciences*, 87(3), 480–496.

Weinhardt, C. & Petry, J. (2024). Contesting China's developing country status: Geoeconomics and the public-private divide in global economic governance. *Chinese Journal of International Politics*, 17(1), 48–74.

Weiss, J. C. & Wallace, J. L. (2021). Domestic politics, China's rise, and the future of the liberal international order. *International Organization*, 75(2), 635–664.

Wiener, A. (2017). A Theory of Contestation – A Concise Summary of Its Argument and Concepts. *Polity*, 49(1), 109–125. www.journals.uchicago.edu/action/showCitFormats?doi=10.1086%2F690100.

Wilke, C. O. (2019). *Fundamentals of data visualization*. Sebastopol: O'Reilly Media.

Williamson, J. (1993). Democracy and the "Washington Consensus". *World Development*, 21(8), 1329–1336.

Wolters, M. E., Barbosa Do Couto, E. & Felício, J. A. (2014). The effects of the global financial crisis on Brazilian banking efficiency. *Innovar*, 24(53), 23–40.

Woods, N. (2008). Whose aid? Whose influence? China, emerging donors and the silent revolution in development assistance. *International Affairs*, 84, 1205–1221.

Woods, N. (2010). *The G20 Leaders and global governance*. University of Oxford, GEG, Working Paper, No. 2010/59.

World Bank. (2021). *A changing landscape: Trends in official financial flows and the aid architecture*. Washington, DC: World Bank Group.

Würdemann, A. I. (2018). The BRICS Contingent Reserve Arrangement: A subversive power against the IMF's conditionality? *Journal of World Investment & Trade*, 19, 570–593.

Xuequin, J. (2022). *Expert calls for BRICS credit rating system*. Chinadaily.com, October 27.

Yu, H. (2017). Motivation behind China's "One Belt, One Road" initiatives and establishment of the Asian Infrastructure Investment Bank. *Journal of Contemporary China*, 26(105), 353–368.

Zeitz, A. O. (2021). Emulate or differentiate? *The Review of International Organizations*, 16(2), 265–292.

Zhu, Z. (2018). Going global 2.0: China's growing investment in the west and its impact. *Asian Perspective*, 42(2), 159–182.

Zysman, J. (1994). How institutions create historically rooted trajectories of growth. *Industrial & Corporate Change*, 4(1), 243–283.

Funding statement

This research was funded by the German Research Foundation / Deutsche Forschungsgemeinschaft (grant no.: 446618653).

The open access publication of this book was funded by the Open Access Publication Fund of Goethe University Frankfurt am Main.

Economics of Emerging Markets

Bruno S. Sergi
Harvard University

Editor Bruno S. Sergi is an Instructor at Harvard University, an Associate of the Harvard University Davis Center for Russian and Eurasian Studies and Harvard Ukrainian Research Institute. He is the Academic Series Editor of the Cambridge *Elements in the Economics of Emerging Markets* (Cambridge University Press), a co-editor of the *Lab for Entrepreneurship and Development* book series, and associate editor of *The American Economist*. Concurrently, he teaches International Economics at the University of Messina, Scientific Director of the Lab for Entrepreneurship and Development (LEAD), and a co-founder and Scientific Director of the International Center for Emerging Markets Research at RUDN University in Moscow. He has published over 150 articles in professional journals and twenty-one books as author, co-author, editor, and co-editor.

About the Series

The aim of this Elements series is to deliver state-of-the-art, comprehensive coverage of the knowledge developed to date, including the dynamics and prospects of these economies, focusing on emerging markets' economics, finance, banking, technology advances, trade, demographic challenges, and their economic relations with the rest of the world, as well as the causal factors and limits of economic policy in these markets.

Cambridge Elements $\overline{\overline{}}$

Economics of Emerging Markets

Elements in the Series

A full series listing is available at: www.cambridge.org/EEM

Printed in the United States
by Baker & Taylor Publisher Services